Time to Stand

by Fred Lopez

www.FredJLopez.com

Praise for *Time to Stand*

"Many people today mourn over present struggles in our society as well as the trajectory that promises more difficulty ahead. The bigger challenge of our day is how to turn the tide. What will offer hope, healing, and a full life in the years ahead? *Time to Stand* offers a rare, and practical, answer to that question. Fred Lopez writes from experience as one serving on the front lines of today's culture. Knowing him as I do, I can say he is a man who practices what he preaches. Fred lives what he challenges us to do in *Time to Stand*. But beware, as this book calls us, not only agree but to take action— to stand! May Fred's call inspire many to influence our day in God's direction for His glory."

— Roy Gruber
Senior Pastor, Washington Heights Church

"I cannot deny that my heart was truly awakened and felt transformed. God's truth seeps through the pages and if your heart is open you will catch it. God is reviving his people and I refuse to miss kingdom opportunities! This book will truly inspire you to make that move and take the stand!"

— Sharon Lopez
Bible Teacher/Discipleship Director/Business Executive

"We live in challenging times. Believers in America are being tested in ways previous generations were not. *Time to Stand* is a powerful tool to help you not only endure, but flourish in the days ahead."

— Steven Dyer
Bible Teacher/Author/Missionary

"Fred Lopez and his wife Janet are a powerhouse couple in the kingdom of our loving God. Their ministry began as pastors of an inner-city church and has grown into a national and international ministry. Their ministry is one of hope for individuals, families, cities and nations. *Time to Stand* is written with a profound hope and determination for change. I pray, as I know Fred does, that this book will bring all who read it a new determination to see hope rise within us all again. As hope rises, I pray a new purity, a new passion, and your placement for such a time as this."

—— Jo Ann Crawford
Team Leader & Outreach Coordinator, Freedom's Fire Ministry

"Apostle Fred Lopez has written a much needed book on the kind of leadership the Body of Christ and the nation need at this point in history! He comprehensively presents the major factors of good and godly leadership. He makes a very strong case, one of the best I have heard, that integrity in the leader is more important than the leader's gifts and abilities. King Solomon would agree! We find these words of wisdom in Proverbs 20:28: 'Good leadership is built on love and truth, for kindness and integrity are what keep leaders in their position of trust'. (The Passion Bible).

Fred reminds his leaders that the highest model of leadership is found in the Lord Jesus Christ. That model, of course, is developed out of a mindset of servanthood. Jesus taught and modeled that the leader was the servant of all. Fred makes an insightful point when he tells us a leader is also a disciple, i.e., an ongoing learner of the ways of Jesus. Jesus told His disciples that were to continue in His Word. Continual learning is for all leaders and all followers in The Kingdom!

He also documents from Paul's writings all the characteristics of good and godly character (I Timothy 3:1-7). This is not theory; this is what the Apostle has learned in his ministry. He wants to be certain that Timothy, his spiritual son, is well informed on the matter.

While there is so much more in this excellent and readable book, I will conclude by sharing another vital truth concerning good leadership: leaders need to be a part of a team of leaders. After all, God Himself is a Team, the dream Team—Father, Son, and Holy Spirit. We find this pattern of team leadership in the Church of the book of Acts. The church at Antioch modeled this. In Acts 13:1-4, we read of the five leaders there who prayed together, heard the Holy Spirit together, and commissioned and sent a team together to extend the Kingdom of God in the Mediterranean world.

As leaders go, so goes the Body of Christ, and as the Body of Christ goes, so goes the nation!

I recommend this volume by my friend and colleague in ministry. May its readership be vast!"

Jim Hodges
Founder and President
Federation of Ministers and Churches, International

[Copyright page]

Contents

Foreword

Time to Stand is a book that serves as a current-day trumpet call to the body of Christ. Fred Lopez invites the reader to take an honest look at the current status of the culture and then respond to each challenge by thinking and acting biblically. Using the scriptures, some history, and even a few stories, Fred engages the heart and mind of each person to journey with him on a pathway of discovery to change the course of our nation's future.

Fred Lopez is a man whose passion for the Lord, His people, and for the Kingdom motivates him to fully engage in the Lord's work. He is able to stand tall as a companion with other leaders yet he always takes time to bend down to serve those in need. He brings biblical perspective and practical solutions to the lives of those to whom he ministers. *Time to Stand* adds yet another dimension to Fred's ministry of bringing transformation to people and to culture.

— Dr. Patti Amsden
Bible Teacher/Prophet/Author

Acknowledgments

I am grateful to God for His hand and presence in my heart and my family. Thank You, Lord, for revealing Your deep love for me anew every day. Your love for me binds my soul to You and drives me to follow You with my life. Thank You for allowing me to serve Your kingdom.

A special thanks to my wonderful wife for your unwavering support in every journey the Lord has taken us! You are truly a gift from God's hand. I look forward to many wonderful years growing together, living our fullest life together, and loving you the way Jesus does.

Also, to my amazing children and spiritual children. You are as precious as gold to me. I am proud of you, and I will always treasure who you are. You are God's gift to me and my gift to the world.

A special dedication to my dear friend Lalo, who passed on to be with Jesus because of complications with COVID-19. Lalo's life was a bright shooting star across a dark world. He had a deep impact on so many people in such a short time. He was the most humble, gracious, and patient person I've ever met. Lalo's heart seemed void of the things I wrestle with daily. His selfless life helped me see a deeper meaning of Scripture. He gave so much grace to the most difficult people. And he always put his own needs last.

"But many who are the greatest now will be least important then, and those who seem least important now will be the greatest then." But now, God has put Lalo first in the kingdom.

Lalo, you were one of the good ones. The rarest kind of friend and brother. I will cherish our memories forever. Your life makes me want to be a better man. I can only hope to take a stand for Jesus the way you did. Until we meet again, my friend, I'll do my best to "Give 'em heaven." In Jesus' name! Thank You, Lord, for allowing me to be part of Lalo's precious life.

Lord, my life's honor is to play a small part within Your wondrous plans of freedom and justice. I pray that every person reading this book sees the depths of Your heart and endless love buried within every page. Give each reader a desire to truly know You as our loving Father. Touch the deepest place within each soul and propel them into a life that follows You to the very ends of themselves.

Introduction

We are living in rare and challenging times, to say the least. Death and wickedness are occurring all around the world. Although the current tragedies, wars, evil, and pandemics are not new, it seems unprecedented to see so much of it happening at once. It appears as if things are going from bad to worse.

God's church is being stretched and forced to grow. The church's response to this moment could make or break our country as we know it today. In fact, I believe we have the opportunity to be part of God's biggest plans to change the course of the world for Jesus.

Time to Stand examines the condition of our culture. You will be taken on a journey to find what's wrong in the most influential institutions and systems that are part of our everyday culture (i.e., church, family, education, business, government, arts/entertainment, and media/social media). Many evangelical leaders today call these cultural elements the Seven Mountains of Culture, or the Seven

Mountains of Influence. We will not get into these particular teachings; however, we will dive into the heart of what's wrong in each of these cultural elements. As we do, you will see the influence they have in our everyday lives.

Before we can find the solution to our corrupt systems and institutions, we must first understand the root of the evil intentions behind the corruption. Eliminating the root of our issues will resolve the wickedness they create. The last thing we need is a temporary solution to a deep seeded problem.

Time to Stand combines biblical revelation with practical solutions, providing a pathway to change the course of our nation's future. This is not just another book about cultural reformation. You will learn how the corruption of our hearts have led to the moral decline within each element of our culture.

This journey will help you discover your own heart's condition in the most hidden places, where you will confront and conquer your internal obstacles. Along this journey, you will begin moving forward toward your most significant destiny in God's kingdom. More importantly, you will discover how your destiny ties in with God's ultimate purposes for our nation to be a beacon of light for the entire world to see the goodness of Jesus Christ. When I talk about your destiny, I'm talking about the reason you were born and God's unique and important purpose for your life during this unusual time we find ourselves living in.

Time to Stand is for the young and seasoned alike. It's for Christians who are both new to the faith and experienced leaders. You will find direction through simple revelation of truth with a historical perspective. The truths in this book are a biblical revelation of God's commands and His timing for you to stand up and set a godly standard for truth, justice, and righteousness, which are the three kingdom pillars a nation must stand on. These pillars are essential for any country to live under God's protection and His blessings.

This book will help every believer understand their obligation to Jesus for realigning our culture and society. You will gain practical ways to make a God-sized difference now, by advancing biblical Christianity, thereby, advancing the kingdom of God.

Stand up, take the journey and you will rise to new unimaginable levels of effectiveness. You will become more useful to God for His purposes. This book is for every man, woman, and child who desires to partner with God during His most significant moment we have ever seen on earth. Your destiny is calling you to take your rightful place in God's kingdom.

This is your *time to stand*!

1

A Falling Nation

We have arrived at a pivotal point in our nation's history. The weight of God's judgment is growing heavy on our nation. Sin and evil plagues every corner of our society like a cancer that is rotting us out. The atrocities of death, destruction, and despair are touching every family and affecting our personal lives. The darkness seems to be surrounding us, trying to slowly squeeze the life from our nation's soul.

Our nation's evil ways are piled high, and our sin goes deep. Our society seems dangerously close to the point of no return with God. We may be at the most critical moment in the history of our nation!

However, there is another story playing out. God has another plan in motion. We are seeing God's Spirit move in ways never witnessed in our land. Within the underbelly of America's darkest and most hopeless places, a spiritual tsunami has begun sweeping the land. It's a collision of two worlds that has forced us to a crossroads. We stand at the brink of these two extremes. The precipice of two futures—a dangerous path or a blessed future.

One path ends in the collapse of our nation, with rubble and billows of smoke on the horizon. Eternal death and destruction for millions of souls.

The other path leads to a redeemed people with freedom anchored to our souls and God's favor shining on our lives. This path will make us a beacon of hope for the entire world to witness God's mercy and His relentless passion to save a people from certain self-destruction. Our fate lies within our own choices. Choices that could unleash God's grace and power, creating a sound that trumpets the name of Jesus into the atmosphere. A sound loud enough for the world to hear.

Which will we choose? This could be the church's greatest moment. God's church can either seize this God-moment or cower in fear.

We have arrived at a moment in time where we need to take a stand against the corruption and injustices plaguing our society. The horrors occurring in our cities and families are unspeakable. We are legalizing evil ways and we consider acceptable things that are an abomination to the very nature of our Creator.

It is *not* the moment to shrink back or sit on the sidelines hoping everything will change. This is your moment to fight. We must fight for our families, our future, our God-given dreams, and a new hope for a new tomorrow for the next generation. If this stirs you, then you were made for this moment.

Isaiah 60:1-2 fits this moment perfectly: "Arise, shine, for your light has come, and the glory of the Lord rises upon you. See, darkness covers the earth and thick darkness is over the peoples, but the Lord rises upon you and His glory appears over you."

This is the church's defining hour. It's the furnace where God's heroes are forged. Your greatest opportunity to make a mark for His kingdom in the story of God's people.

I believe that God is scouring the earth for believers who are willing to stand up and face the adversity of this moment— Christians who are willing to courageously stand for truth, justice, and righteousness. I can almost hear God speaking Psalm 94:16, and saying, "Who will rise up for me against the wicked? Who will take a stand for me against the evildoers?"

All the while, our country seems to be turning its back on Jesus and has become indignant toward Jesus and His ways. Our society is intolerant of the mere *name* of Jesus. Popularity has grown to take a stand for smoking marijuana, announcing your homosexuality, or murdering full-term babies than it is to say Jesus' name, stay a virgin until you are married or stand for God's truths.

All of these things are happening while Satan is spilling blood from the innocent in unspeakable ways. For example, the rate of abortion has exceeded 63 million babies in the U.S. since 1973 when Roe v. Wade was enacted. And the rate of babies aborted worldwide since 1980 is a staggering 1.6 billion according to www.numberofabortions.com.

The level of genocide is beyond biblical proportions, and the most sickening thing about it is that we have become numb to it. Our lack of action against it speaks loudly to God and says, we are comfortable with it.

One of the hidden tragedies concerning abortion is the number of mothers devasted in the wake of this wave of death. In the face of our political battles over aborting unborn children, there are millions of mothers deceived into thinking life is just a fleshy blob with a pro-choice consequence. Now, those mothers must live with the horrors of a soul-crushing lie.

What about them? Who is crying out for the silenced mothers? Better yet, who is reaching out to the countless mothers desperate for healing? *The Lord will bless those who stand up for the weak.* Psalm 41:1 says, "Blessed are those who have regard for the weak."

Blood is being spilled on our nation's soil. The blood is deep, and our hands are covered with it. No city is safe. No mother is safe. No child is safe.

Let's take a brief look at the increasing corruption in our society. At the heart of corruption is idolatry, and it has become deeply engrained within every aspect of our culture at every socioeconomic level. Our appetite for power and money has become the cornerstone of our culture, our governmental systems, and our business practices.

Our nation has become more dependent on our wealth and military force than we depend on God. Full-term babies are being murdered in the same hospitals obligated to protect our health. Transgender surgery for preteen children is encouraged and celebrated, while it has become intolerable for our children to pray in school.

Marijuana dispensaries have become legal, and alcoholism is commonplace, while heroin, methamphetamine, and synthetic narcotics demolish lives in millions of families.

Many big cities have grown numb to violence and murder, while prescription drugs play a silent role in crossing boundaries into every socioeconomic neighborhood to ravage the rest of our society. Even our children's minds are unsafe. They are being bombarded with the everchanging music, movies and media shaping them with evil and wicked things. The boundaries of "acceptable and good" are continuously challenged and redefined.

It doesn't end with all those things. The culture of our corporate world and business practices are growing more cutthroat. It has become the norm to cheat, steal and lie to exploit other companies, take advantage of the weak-minded or less fortunate, and use tactics with an "anything goes" mentality to gain market share. It all stems from greed and a gluttonous appetite for wealth.

Additionally, our political system is corrupted by the power of influential people and wealthy companies that will do anything for the sake of their money hungry self-interests. Too many of our politicians have become puppets, too scared to stand for the best interests of our nation's future or the poor and weak. Many of our nation's leaders lack the spine to speak their true stance on important issues, in fear of losing supporters and votes.

Meanwhile, terrorism redefines how we fight wars. Terrorists are becoming more and more extreme. They detonate bombs in public places like the site of the Boston Marathon bombing and they crash planes into the World Trade Center. It's as if God has continued pulling away His hand of protection to get our attention and turn back to Him.

There should not be any doubt we are under God's judgment. Our nation's sins are growing deeper by the hour. We are constantly inventing new ways to sin against God by exploiting others and killing each other. And it's happening on our watch!

If there ever was a Time to Stand, it is now.

It does not mean the entire world is coming to an end, just because the U.S. is getting worse. Powerful countries from the past have been through much worse, committing crimes against humanity in unspeakable ways. Some simple research will show the numerous countries that started out good, became a superpower and ended up imploding from moral decline. Other countries have suffered from evil dictators who committed genocide within their own country, and even worse forms of genocide to their surroundings countries. Nonetheless, our country finds itself at a historic moment. A moment that goes beyond the enemy's tactics to flood our news media outlets and bombard our minds.

There is something more sinister at work behind the scenes trying to crush our nation, and it is not a conspiracy theory. It's the culmination of countless tiny steps of compromise that have taken us off the path of God's ways. We have allowed the sinful desires lurking within the darkest places of our heart to escape into the reality of our world.

Many people ask, "Where is God in all of this?" While it is true that Jesus will come again to eradicate all sin and evil from the planet, the time has not come yet. For now, it is the church's responsibility.

This is a God-moment for the church to stand up and become the moral compass of our nation. We must take our rightful place as the conscience for the soul of America. Jesus created the church to be the head and not the tail. We are supposed to lead and not follow the ways of this world.

We possess the key to unlock God's blessings into the earth and break the curses off an entire nation. Jesus created the church especially for moments like this.

If we consider ourselves followers of Jesus, we must make good on our covenant with Christ to stand for justice, truth, and righteousness. We must stop turning a blind eye to it.

Pastor Sam Rodriguez, Author of "Be Light" often says, "There is no such thing as comfortable Christianity." Jesus said it more plainly, in Matthew 16:24: "Whoever wants to be my disciple must deny themselves and take up their cross and follow me." That scripture means we are supposed to put our lives on the line for His cause.

I've heard some Christians say, "Well, that's not my calling." Or "I don't feel led to do that." Another verse quoting Jesus' own words emphasizes our responsibility and hits it home best: "Whoever does not take up their cross and follow me is not worthy of me" (Matthew 10:38).

I chose these words from Jesus as a stark wake-up call about the responsibility of every believer to change our world.

If you take time to read the New Testament, with an eye towards the church's early history, you will see countless people who put their lives on the line. In fact, if you read world history where demonic tyranny existed, you will find brave Christians who put their lives on the line for truth and justice.

The fact is, we must face the issues of our day head-on, both with our voices and our actions. There is no choice in the matter. Jesus invented the church and established her to be a beacon of light so the entire world will know His name and follow His ways. We are supposed to raise a banner for Him and stand up for others who cannot stand for themselves. Jesus laid down His life on the cross, for a broken world, and He expects us to follow Him in the same way.

The remainder of this book takes you on a journey through the soul of America. We will dive into every part of our culture to discover how we went wrong in each part of it. Then, we will explore practical ways that every believer can do their part and change our world.

The goal of this book is to unlock the power of God's Spirit onto the earth, through the destiny of God's church. You will find that we possess the power of God's Spirit within us to turn things around. When you combine that power with a willingness to live our lives for His cause, God will unleash His life-giving power that changes everything plaguing our world.

2

God's Judgment

Before we jump into the ways we can help change things, it's important that we understand where our country stands with God. We need to understand what's happening to our nation from God's viewpoint, so we will better understand how we can go about repairing the damage. Now I am not God, nor do I know the mind of God. We will merely look at things from a biblical perspective, which reveals both the mind and heart of God.

We all know times are changing for the worse. It's not hard to figure that out. But there is a more important question. *Why is it happening?* One reason is that there's a cosmic battle occurring as we speak, and there is more at stake than we realize. This cosmic battle started in the Garden of Eden, and it has been heating up ever since. And there should be no doubt that God needs more from His church than we are currently giving Him, because the soul of America is at stake.

America has a big hole in the middle of her soul, and it appears she's trying to fill it with wickedness and hatred for God's ways. It stems from a never-ending appetite for wealth, power, and personal pleasures.

The Bible gives us insight into many of our nation's deepest issues in Jeremiah 7:6-8: "If you do not oppress the foreigner, the fatherless or the widow and do not shed innocent blood in this place, and if you do not follow other gods to your own harm, then I will let you live in this place, in the land I gave your ancestors for ever and ever."

This single verse touches on many of our deepest issues, such as, the way we treat foreigners, human trafficking, fatherlessness, and abortion, and it says if we follow His ways we will remain in our land. Conversely, if we refuse to follow His ways, the verse implies He will not allow us to stay in this land.

Look how Jeremiah 5:27-29 also applies to our country. "'They have become rich and powerful and have grown fat and sleek. Their evil deeds have no limit; they do not seek justice. They do not promote the case of the fatherless; they do not defend the just cause of the poor. Should I not punish them for this?' declares the Lord. 'Should I not avenge myself on such a nation as this?'"

These verses seem as if God is speaking directly to us right now, in this moment and at this time. His words are warnings that must be taken to heart. When will we listen to God's warnings? The tragic events of 9-11 did not turn our nation back to God. Will the effects of COVID-19 get our attention focused back on God and our families? Let's dig deeper into God's view of our nation's condition.

There are only a few things that stir God's anger and provoke His wrath toward a nation. It has to do with the way a nation refuses to rely on God and how it mistreats the poor, less fortunate and those who are incapable of defending themselves.

Jesus said the two most important commands are to love God and love others. He said, in Luke 10:27, "'Love the Lord your God with all your heart and with all your soul and with all your strength and with all your mind'; and, 'Love your neighbor as yourself.'"

The first command speaks about loving God, which includes trusting Him and following His ways. God will not tolerate a nation that relies on its wealth, power, and military force instead of relying on God and His ruling power. When a nation becomes dependent upon its own power and wealth, those things become a self-reliant idol. They become more important than God Himself. It is the essence of idolatry, which is a direct sin against God's most important command.

Hosea 10:14 says it best: "Because you have depended on your own strength and on your many warriors, the roar of battle will rise against your people, so that all your fortresses will be devasted." This is a powerful scripture, and it explains the reasons we have so much terrorism within our borders, violence amongst ourselves and receive so much hatred from other countries. It should also serve as a stark wake-up call for each of us.

The second command relates to the way we treat others. God demands that we exercise compassion for the less fortunate, value others and treat everyone fairly and equally in all situations. That command applies to every part of our lives, whether it's our business

15

practices, governmental laws, or the relationships within our families. Loving others puts other people's best interests ahead of our own, regardless of the cost to our egos, our precious time, or our bank accounts.

Jesus will not tolerate corruption or deception for personal gain, especially at the expense of others. Look at Isaiah 61:8: "For I, the Lord, love justice; I hate robbery and wrongdoing."

In this verse, God uses strong words of love and hate. The verses in Hosea and Isaiah should start to reveal God's disdain towards injustice and mistreating others. In fact, Jesus becomes intolerant with a society that continuously disobeys those two foundational commands to love Him and love others. It's a level of disobedience that pushes God's anger over the edge. This is especially true when a society combines it with an attitude of self-reliance on their wealth and power for its safety and security instead of relying on God's sovereign protection.

Disobeying God's two most important commands is the type of moral decline proven to be a cancer that eventually causes every nation to collapse. A nation is incapable of escaping this type of self-destruction using its own power. God's ways and the blood of Jesus provide the only path to fix things. God's words in Micah 5:15 are very clear about where we stand with God. "I will take vengeance in anger and wrath on the nations that have not obeyed me."

Are you still wondering where our country stands with God? Well, we do not need to be biblical scholars, prophets or even the wisest person to figure it out. You can see it for yourself. Let's look at the Bible a little more, for a broader perspective.

We can get a good understanding of where we stand with God by comparing Israel's birth, rise, and fall with America's relationship with God. It will also provide amazing insight into the destiny of America.

I have only listed a few comparisons between Israel and America. The list is not meant to be an exhaustive list. You need to read the Bible and American history for yourself. Then you will see many more comparisons than I'm pointing out.

Here are many ways America and Israel are similar:

- The United States was founded on biblical laws, principles, values, and morals. God and His ways were the foundation of our country.

- God gave us a new land for a fresh start, where we established a covenant with God to follow His ways. In God's faithfulness, He removed us from the tyranny of a godless nation.

- America started out faithful to God, and our country was committed to His laws. We were a people grateful for His grace. His laws were engrained into the fabric of our culture, our government, and our families. God's ways were instilled into our children, and following His laws were passed down to each generation.

- God gave us great favor in everything we did. He even gave us great wealth beyond the rest of the world, with the sole purpose to show the nations God's great blessings come when we follow His ways.

- Like Israel, America was supposed to be a beacon of light and hope for the world. Now our country has become worse than our neighboring nations.

- Israel struggled with issues of foreigners living in their land. They made some of them slaves during the time of King Solomon. It eventually turned into a major civil war that ripped Israel apart at the seams, and they have never been the same since. America also dealt with slavery, which caused a civil war.

- God made Israel the wealthiest country in the world during King Solomon's rule. Then, the pursuit of wealth and power eventually took center stage in the soul of Israel. Israel took refuge in their military power and political alliances. Their selfish ambitions drove them into corruption and injustices against those who are less fortunate, poor, and powerless. These are the most extreme forms of idolatry—a direct sin against God and His most important laws.

- Israel's actions of godlessness were an abomination to God and the world He created. It was an act of defiance of God's grace, even though He had set them free from Egypt's tyranny. Israel removed true worship from the land and replaced it with demonic worship, prostitution, and homosexuality.

- Israel's never-ending appetite for wickedness, wealth, and power drove them mad for more. Their godly morals and values were consumed by the bloodshed of their children and elderly. Their personal pleasures became a cancer that killed their souls.

- The Lord used godless nations to wage war against Israel. He wanted to get their attention to turn them back to Him for refuge. Instead, they created political alliances with godless nations and relied on their military power for protection. It all backfired because of their unfaithfulness and pride.

In summary, the Bible says that the Lord blessed Israel in every way. He gave them a new land, great peace, and unequaled wealth. His intention was to have Israel become a beacon of light to the sinful ways of their surrounding nations. Instead, Israel became worse than their neighbors. Israel was later conquered, and God removed them from their land.

Israel's rise and fall are very similar to America's history and current path. God warned Israel over and over, and He is undoubtedly trying to warn us. We have repaid God's grace with sin; given Him evil for His mercy and corruption for His justice; and we offer Him murder and death instead of righteousness and justice.

Will we follow the same path of downward spiral? Jeremiah 13:14 says, "I will allow no pity or mercy or compassion to keep me from destroying them." One thing is for sure: God cast judgment upon His precious Israel, and He will surely do it to America too.

Perhaps the better question is, are we at the point of no return with God? Well, there are two things we do know for sure. The first is that we absolutely need God's hand to recover our nation from its downward spiral. Second, we know God is merciful and forgiving, and our nation is still intact, which means we still have a chance.

It's common to hear people say, "Where is God in all of this?" Many of our cities and families appear to be falling apart around us. When you watch the news, our nation appears to be unraveling at the seams. Much of the corruption and godlessness from our country's actions convey a message to God that points our collective fingers in God's face, in disdain of His ways. Our society seems determined to live a life emptied of God's blessings, while living entrenched in the curses of His wrath. Simply put, our nation's sins are piled high, and the evil goes deep.

So, next time someone asks the question, "Where is God in all of this?" you will have the answer. God's grace is the only thing holding our nation together. And God is undoubtedly the only answer to get us out of this situation we find ourselves in.

I believe the Holy Spirit is in the middle of it all. He's holding us together, although our actions are ripping apart our country. The same way our country was divided during the presidential elections in 2020. There was chaos, looting, setting cities on fire, killings, violent protesting, fighting between families and strife within the church body. Only God can hold together a nation that seems bent on tearing itself apart.

Although some things seem to be going from bad to worse, we are simultaneously experiencing the most significant move of God in the history of our nation. God's Spirit is moving within the most hopeless hearts like a wildfire. He is reviving people from the most desolate places and calling the most unlikely people to lead the way into a new, hope-filled future. It's as if a new hope is arising from the ashes. A new hope that was forged from the hellfire of their past.

It is exactly the way Jesus works. He uses the weakest to reveal His mighty hand. He uses the worst of sinners to reveal His everlasting goodness.

Do you feel a stirring passion in your heart to be used by the Lord to change your world? Begin to pray. Ask the Holy Spirit to reveal His heart and His plans so you can partner with Him. Take the journey through the remainder of this book, and it will help you find yourself and find your most significant place in God's kingdom.

3

It's Not a Choice

Satan has been feeding our minds with a lie in the American church for decades. He is using a twisted ideal that's called separation of church and state to systematically remove God and His ways from every corner of our culture. This lie says that the church should stay out of the government's business, and the government should stay out of the church's affairs. It's an ideal that's only a half-truth mixed with a twisted deception. The ideal stems from a portion of the First Amendment to the U.S. Constitution, which states, "Congress shall make no law respecting an establishment of religion, or prohibiting the free exercise thereof. . . ."

This portion of the Amendment means that government cannot impose a state mandated religion upon the public. Nor can it place undue restrictions on our religious practices. At the core of the

Amendment is that the church must remain self-governing, and the government cannot govern the church or rule over it.

Somehow, government added an unwritten portion to the First Amendment, without making any changes to it. The twisted lie makes us believe we're not allowed to bring our faith into politics. This lie gave government a false permission to remove God's ways from our politics and policies. This lie has crept into every facet of our systems and institutions. We see it in schools, our workplace, judicial system, and every other place you can think of. Biblical values are being removed from ethical business practices, a biblically centered educational system, and the sacred institution of marriage.

Our society has taken the lie and run with it. Christian children are not allowed to pray in schools. Athletes are frowned upon when they give praise to Jesus or pray during games. We cannot even say the name of Jesus in public without the weight of this lie condemning us. The deception has granted the freedom to operate with corruption and greed, worship whatever god we want and live whatever life we see fit, as long as it has nothing to do with Jesus or the Bible.

We have been deceived with this false premise. A deception that allows our mortal enemy to strip away God's ways from our society. Although there are believers who are faithful to Jesus and His ways, our nation's culture does not hold to biblical values any longer. In other words, our political, business, and educational systems do not value or follow God's ways. When God sees that our culture rejects Jesus and His ways, He judges our entire nation as a whole. It does not mean all believers are sinning or that we will all go to hell. However, it does mean that our entire nation is held responsible for deliberately removing God's fundamental values, morals, and principles from our society. It equates to a deliberate act of disobedience that opens the floodgates for corruption and injustice throughout our culture. Consequently, we become a cursed nation, and our nation suffers the consequences of God's judgement, discipline, and eventually His wrath.

Here's a question that should help you understand God's perspective differently. *Do you think God is okay with deliberate acts of lawlessness and disobedience in a world He created?*

There's another frightful impact on the church that stemmed from the lie about separation of church and state. And in my opinion, it has been the most destructive to the American church and perhaps to our country's future. The demonic lie has convinced much of the church they should stay out of politics and the government's business. It has made the church feel as if we shouldn't even talk about politics or any type of government dealings. As if we live within some sort of churchy bubble with an alternate reality. The reality is the church is responsible for the path of our nation. We are not living in a world that is separated from our nation. America is our land with our people living here, and we have a responsibility to God, our people and the nation God gave us.

In case you're unaware, the church's job is to rule the earth on behalf of God. We are not supposed to passively ignore the bad institutions we have created. Revelations 5:10 says, "You have made

27

them to be a kingdom and priests to serve our God, and they will reign on the earth." More on that in later chapters.

You often hear from Christians who won't get involved with civil or federal governmental issues. Some of them refuse to simply vote because they believe the Bible is against getting involved. Another false belief has convinced many believers that our responsibility to God stops within the walls of our local church or inside our homes. It is a lie that creates an ineffective church, lacking its true identity and ignorant about its true responsibilities to God.

I hope it is becoming a little clearer that one of Satan's tactics is to strip the church of its authority and blind us about our responsibility to lead our nation toward God's ways. The fact is, Satan wants to stop the church from assuming its role in realigning our society's ways with God's ways. Contrary to popular belief, Jesus expects His church to stand against these things plaguing our world and resolve them with compassion, courage, and truth.

Unfortunately, most Christians think their responsibility to Jesus ends when they attend church on Sunday or even after they bring someone to Christ. When we say *yes* to Jesus, we are literally committing our lives to His cause for the advancement of the kingdom of God into every part of the world.

Before we move forward from this important topic, we need to take a step back to understand our responsibility to Jesus with more clarity. This topic is the launching point from which you will be propelled into your proper destiny. Reconciliation and reformation are tied to our identity in Christ. Suffice it to say, understanding our commitment to Jesus is a critical topic of the utmost importance, not only for this book but for your life.

For starters, we must accept the fact that God did not create the earth so Satan could destroy it. He created the earth for mankind, for our future and for us to live with Him. Furthermore, God certainty did not create mankind so Satan could destroy us in the world God created. Our Father took great care when He created this world for us. In fact, He commissioned the angels to carry out His plans for us, caring for us and serving us.

Unfortunately, we are not following God's plans. We never have. Mankind has been living in rebellion against God since Adam and

Eve sinned. Mankind screwed it up back then and we are still screwing it up today.

God clearly communicated His plans and expectations to Adam for all humankind in Genesis 1, which is commonly referred to as the Dominion Mandate in Genesis 1:26-30:

> Then God said, "Let us make mankind in our image, in our likeness, so that they may rule over the fish in the sea and the birds in the sky, over the livestock and all the wild animals, and over all the creatures that move along the ground."
>
> So God created mankind in his own image, in the image of God he created them; male and female he created them.
>
> God blessed them and said to them, "Be fruitful and increase in number; fill the earth and subdue it. Rule over the fish in the sea and the birds in the sky and over every living creature that moves on the ground."
>
> Then God said, "I give you every seed-bearing plant on the face of the whole earth and every tree that has fruit with seed in it. They will be yours for food. And to all the beasts of the earth and all the birds in the sky and all the creatures that move along the ground—everything that has the breath of life in it—I give every green plant for food." And it was so.

Then Jesus gave us another command in Matthew 28:18-20, which is commonly referred to as the Great Commission:

> Then Jesus came to them and said, "All authority in heaven and on earth has been given to me. Therefore go and make disciples of all nations, baptizing them in the name of the Father and of the Son and of the Holy Spirit, and teaching them to obey everything I have commanded you. And surely I am with you always, to the very end of the age."

Jesus's words above command us to follow God's original mandate. But this time, Jesus included expectations that require us to fix the things we broke and realign our ways back to God's original Dominion Mandate.

Take some time to study the scriptures in Genesis 1 and Matthew 28 carefully to understand how they align. God's commands in those two scriptures transcend the pages of this book. They are key and foundational to our purpose on this earth. We will briefly review these two commands separately to understand God's expectation from us. Then, we will tie them together.

We will look at the Dominion Mandate first, which is God's original command for us to rule the earth and everything in it. Here are some key phrases from the Dominion Mandate in Genesis 1:26-30: "Then God said, 'Let us make mankind in our image, in our likeness, so that they may rule.' . . . So God created mankind in His own image. . . . He created them; male and female. . . . God blessed them and said to them, 'Be fruitful and increase in number; fill the earth and subdue it. Rule . . . everything that has the breath of life in it. . . . And it was so.'"

Within this scripture are God's purposes for creating mankind. We are supposed to rule God's world according to the way He wants it done. Essentially, we are His representatives on earth, just as we are ambassadors for Jesus. Our responsibility is to manage or steward this world and everything in it.

Although we messed things up, God's command still stands true today. We are supposed to create a society with a culture that has God's laws at the center of everything we do. His mandate for us is to run the earth *like* He would, by representing Him in everything we do.

When you combine that scripture with the Ten Commandments, it becomes clear that we are supposed to manage the earth, its resources, the animals, etc., and create loving families with godly parents—husbands and wives who love and respect each other. We should raise our children to love God through our actions and examples, rely on Him alone, and put the needs of others first. We are to instill godly values and morals into everything our hands build in a way that glories God and benefits everyone around us. His Word does not come back void, nor does it change. His Word stands—

yesterday, today, and tomorrow. God's Word will fulfill its purposes on earth.

The conditions of today's world and in particular America should start becoming clearer by now. God did not create the earth so Satan could run it and destroy us in it. God created it for His creation to live and rule over, while we follow God's ways and remain in close relationships with Him.

However, sin came into the picture fast. Adam allowed it into this world; we have also allowed it into our lives; and a sinful culture that opposes God and His laws was created and spread throughout our nation. Just as Adam created an opening for Satan, we created an opening for him within our society.

Adam's decision to disobey God invited death and destruction into our world, and we have been paying for it ever since. Sin moved swiftly into Adam and Eve's family, beginning with the loss of their son Abel, who was murdered by his brother Cain. It was the first murder on earth, and it marked the beginning of bloodshed that has plagued the entire history of mankind. And it all happened on Adam's watch.

The U.S. has its own history of bloodshed. Bloodshed has filled our nation's soil for centuries— from slavery and the civil war to hate crimes, gang killings, human trafficking, abortions, serial killers, and on and on. Each of us has been doing our part to make things worse throughout every generation. In fact, blood is still being shed today, and this time it is happening on our watch. If we don't take a stand now, what will things look like in twenty or thirty years?

There are critical questions we must answer within our own souls: When will we get our fill of destruction and corruption? What will we allow on our watch?

Our decision to remain silent is a choice that says we agree and support the evil and corruption. What is holding you back? Is it fear, lack of deep concern, or a feeling of helplessness? Or is it some philosophical belief that keeps you from confronting our nation's issues head-on? Either way, it is a decision to turn a blind eye to the issues plaguing our society. Our decision translates into an intentional act to disregard God's commands. As you already know, we are accountable to God for our actions and our inactions, and we will eventually give an account for our lives when we meet Jesus face-to-face.

This quote from Dr. Martin Luther King Jr. says it all: "He who passively accepts evil is as much involved in it as he who helps to perpetrate it. He who accepts evil without protesting against it is really cooperating with it."

Now let's discuss the Great Commission in a little more detail. It also contains God's original purposes for creating mankind. But this time, Jesus put His blood on it because the world is fallen and humanity's relationship with God is broken.

Fortunately, Jesus came into our broken and fallen world and provided a way to change everything. His death and resurrection re-established rightful ownership of the entire earth for all mankind. Jesus' sacrifice provided a way for every human being to unite with our loving Father for an eternal relationship. Jesus gave us a new start: a restart for all things broken.

After Jesus sacrificed Himself on the cross for us and rose from the dead, He empowered us to fulfill God's original mandate. He gave us God's original Dominion Mandate again. This time, He added a little something to it. Look at the scripture in Matthew 28:18-20, where Jesus says, "All authority in heaven and on earth has been given to me. Therefore go and make disciples of all nations, baptizing them in the name of the Father and of the Son and of the Holy Spirit, and teaching them to obey everything I have commanded you. And surely I am with you always, to the very end of the age."

Jesus is basically saying, "I have the power to restore order in the earth. Now I am giving you the power to fix the problems you created, through My grace, My blood, and the power of My Spirit." And when you read it within the context of Matthew 16:18-19 it says, "And on this rock I will build my church, and the gates of Hades will not overcome it. I will give you the keys of the kingdom of heaven; whatever you bind on earth will be bound in heaven, and whatever you loose on earth will be loosed in heaven."

Through this verse, Jesus gave us His power and the authority to release His plans and purposes into our communities and nation. Now you should begin to see that the Great Commission is Jesus' command to take back what Satan stole and change our society's culture, with God's laws at the center. It also tells us how to realign our broken and fallen world with God's plans and purposes. Here are a couple of highlights from the two scriptures we just reviewed.

- Jesus is King of all things in heaven and on earth.
- Tell everyone about Jesus—what He has done for you and the good news of salvation and hope for a new future if we love Him with our life.
- Create disciples who follow Jesus with their lives.
- Teach others how to follow God's ways in everything they do, especially in our homes.
- Jesus' blood empowers believers to realign all the evil and cursed ways that have corrupted mankind.

Be sure you do not overlook a critical element in Matthew 28:20. It's the part that says, "teaching them to obey everything I have commanded you." This portion of Scripture goes beyond changing your personal lifestyle. It says to teach and show others in every nation how to follow God's ways. Jesus is saying we need to realign the systems, structures, culture, and ways that oppose God's ways of living.

37

When we follow God's commands, we can rest assured that God is faithful. He will come through on His end to bless our nation and our future generations. Jesus is asking for a high level of obedience and multiplication.

Here are a few practical examples that will help you understand the depth of Jesus' command.

Say we lead someone to Jesus who was an addict, an alcoholic, a gang banger, or just a plain violent person. Maybe they have only seen that type of lifestyle growing up. Their mindset has been conditioned and deceived into believing that it is normal to live a dysfunctional lifestyle that is highly destructive to themselves and everyone around them. The new believer may not know any other way of life. It's their normal.

Consequently, we must teach them a whole new way of living. They may need to get a job and stop stealing, cheating, or selling drugs. They need to learn how to become a godly father, mother, or spouse to ensure their brokenness doesn't infect their children and household. In other words, their ways need to be realigned with

God's ways. I call it living a blessed life instead of living a cursed life.

Let's take another simple but powerful example. Say we lead a CEO to the Lord. Our new believer conducts unethical business practices. She takes advantage of her customers and overcharges them for her company's services. She mistreats her employees and underpays them. She even cheats on her taxes to keep money that legally belongs to the government. Our new convert's business principles and personal values are corrupt and self-centered. Her ideals of cutthroat business practices drive her to do anything for wealth, power, and a false version of success. Her business practices are corrupt on several levels.

Anyone can plainly see that we must teach our new believer a better way of life. A life aligned with God's ways that releases God's eternal blessings into her life, her employees, and everyone she does business with. Before God's blessings can be released into her life, her heart needs to be recalibrated along with her personal values and business practices. Her old ways are in direct conflict with God's ways.

For example, she must change the way she does business by providing her customers with a high value product for a competitive price that is fair and favors her customers. Her employees need to be paid a fair wage according to their job responsibilities and previous work experience, along with regular raises, benefits, etc. Our new believer must change her crooked accounting practices and start paying the appropriate taxes. Not to mention she must pay tithes consistently and use some of her business profits to pour back into God's kingdom.

In summary, the CEO must now become ethical, honest, fair, and generous. These are kingdom qualities that reflect the character of our loving Father. It takes deep trust in God to follow His ways. It's often a blind trust that believes God will prosper your business and your life in the deepest ways. A type of trust that puts God's ways and other people's needs ahead of your own personal desires for wealth or success, thereby creating the correct biblical view for success and a new pathway toward eternal blessings.

We could use examples from all sorts of people working in any type of job, such as a politician, musician, movie director, actor, news reporter, football player, coach, lawyer, doctor, educator, etc. Imagine for a moment how someone from each of these professions could change the way they operate. Then you will start to realize the potential depth of influence each person could have amongst their peers and eventually, what the overall impact would be throughout their respective industries.

We possess great potential to impact every aspect of our culture. With a united effort aligned with God's ways and purposes, we hold the power of God inside us to impact every aspect of our world.

These examples should start revealing how our society's current culture, systems, and ways of thinking can be realigned with God's ways. Hopefully, you have begun realizing that Jesus' Great Commission goes beyond creating new believers. We are supposed to create disciples that are world-changers. I know many of you have heard this statement before. Hopefully, it is beginning to take on a much broader meaning.

Taking it further, the scripture from Jesus' Great Commission says we must take a stand to undo corruption and wickedness. We must each get involved and do our part to change the core of corrupt systems and wicked ways of thinking. Of course, it all begins with our willingness to allow the Holy Spirit to confront and realign the deepest places within our own corrupt hearts. Because our hearts are the root from which all corruption stems.

I hope you now see how crucial it is to understand Jesus' commission in its entirety. Understanding the depth of Jesus' purposes allows us to grasp His bigger plans for restoration. A deeper understanding allows us to set our sights higher, toward giving Jesus all the things He is asking from us. This puts us in a better place to partner with Jesus on a more impactful level, making ourselves more useful to Him concerning the things He has planned and purposed.

To take it deeper, the moment we accept Jesus we enter a lifetime covenant with Him. We become obligated to follow Him to the ends of the earth, and ultimately, to the ends of ourselves. Doing anything less puts us in jeopardy of breaking that covenant.

Look at what it says in Matthew 16:24-25: "Whoever wants to be my disciple must deny themselves and take up their cross and follow me. For whoever wants to save their life will lose it, but whoever loses their life for me will find it."

Jesus' commands are not optional. Anything less is disobedience, and disobeying God's Word is a sin. Our disobedience could be a result of deep-rooted internal issues, or it might be a result of ignorance. Either way, it is still disobedience. Unfortunately for us, we do not have a choice, and our opinions have no bearing on God's truths or the consequences thereof.

We will dive deeper into the personal rooted issues that often get in the way of obedience, in later chapters. For now, we merely want to make a connection. The moral decline of individuals within a country will always lead to the moral decline of an entire country.

The Bible is clear that a nation's continual disobedience will eventually end in its demise. You may or may not agree at this point, but it is a fact that every single nation in the history of mankind has collapsed after they turned their backs on God's ways. Doing so creates a moral decline that results in an incurable disease called sin. It happened to Israel that we read in the Bible, and it can happen to us. Hopefully you are beginning to understand the reason we

43

emphasized the portion of scripture in Matthew 28:19-20 of the Great Commission. "Go and make disciples of all nations…teaching them to obey everything I commanded you."

Jeremiah 12:17 addresses it very clearly: "'But if any nation does not listen, I will completely uproot and destroy it,' declares the Lord."

Now the connection between God's Dominion Mandate and Jesus' Great Commission should be much clearer. The first was God's original command for us to rule the earth on His behalf, according to the way He does things. The second empowered us with God's Spirit to change everything back to God's original plan—to exchange the curses for blessings, hopelessness for a new future, and brokenness for healing and wholeness. Jesus made it possible for us through the blood He shed on the cross.

When we begin to grasp the fundamental truths in this chapter, our mindset about kingdom building will be changed forever. We will start to see the entire world as our pulpit. Needless to say, it is critical for us to spend time studying the Bible to understand this chapter more fully. This subject of God's expectations is the launching point for the remainder of this book. In fact, it is the

launching point for God's most significant purposes in our life.

4

Time to Stand

By now, you may be starting to wonder what you can or should do to make a difference. Or better yet, what God expects from you at this point in your life. This chapter will show you the extraordinary things God has done through the most ordinary people who often came from the most hopeless situations.

In fact, Jesus created the church body to carry hope, stand against injustices, and change the course of a self-destructive world. If sin is a cancer, God's church is the answer. God created you for the moment in which we live.

God's wonderful ways are masterful at using ordinary people to do the most heroic things. God loves using the weak to overcome the strong. He uses the most unlikely people to lead the charge, especially when the odds are stacked the highest. God loves to let His goodness shine by using His miracle-working power to pull off the unthinkable victory using people from the most broken pasts.

God has a way of revealing His deep grace through His overcoming power.

A review of history will reveal countless ordinary Christians who took a stand against evil leaders, horrific situations, and cruel injustices against the innocent. Ordinary men and women, just like us, have put their lives on the line against horrific atrocities of their day. And they did it against all odds while facing financial ruin, imprisonment, death, or worse. There are certain attributes that launched ordinary people into a heroic status of Christian folklore. Those attributes from seemingly heroic Christians include their willingness to endure suffering and extreme persecution to advance God's agenda.

There you go. Now you know one of the secret ingredients from ordinary people who loved Jesus and were willing to risk death for their biblical beliefs and values. They embraced suffering and persecution as an honor. It is an entirely different mindset toward Christianity from what we might think of today.

Changing your perspective will redefine your entire mindset. It is a deeper commitment that we, as Christians, need to have grafted into our DNA. It's the difference maker. Our first step of turning our nation back to God and His ways is to change our mindset. I have heard Francis Chan, author of Crazy Love, Letters to The Church and Until Unity, say that one of the things that made the first century church an "unstoppable force" is the way they embraced suffering and persecution.

If we possess this one single attribute, nothing can stop us. Satan himself cannot stop anyone willing to lay down their life for God's plans. Jesus showed us the way, and we are supposed to follow Him. This fearless mindset removes Satan's power of fear and manipulation from our life. He becomes disarmed because he has nothing with which he can use to hold us back or hold us down.

We are honored to follow Jesus, and it is a privilege to endure persecution for His cause. This is the first step toward taking back everything Satan stole from us and from God's kingdom. We will dive deeper into this subject during the latter chapters of this book.

For now, you can read about some of the dedicated Christians in the Bible. A couple of common names that come to mind are Stephen, Paul, and Peter. These were ordinary men who put their lives on the line by challenging and opposing corrupt religious and political systems that were unrighteous, ungodly, and power hungry. God used the courage and commitment of a few common believers to spread the gospel and create a new global church. We will look at a few examples of how God used ordinary people to do extraordinary things.

One of those ordinary people was Peter. He was a commercial fisherman who made lots of mistakes after accepting Jesus into his life. However, there was one specific moment in Peter's life when he had an epic failure. It was the night before Jesus was crucified, Peter told Jesus he would die for Him. A few short hours later, Jesus was imprisoned, and Peter denied knowing Christ. It was probably the lowest moment in Peter's life.

But Jesus didn't give up on him. Given a second chance, Peter's commitment to Jesus grew deeper than he could have ever imagined. As a result, Jesus was able to use Peter to shake up the world. In fact, Peter later endured terrible suffering and persecution to advance Christianity into a corrupt and sinful world. He was beaten and thrown in jail several times for preaching about Jesus and teaching people to follow God's ways.

Peter's entire mindset was changed by Jesus' love. You can see it in a conversation Peter had with the religious leaders who imprisoned him in Acts 4:18: "Then they called them [Peter and John] in again and commanded them not to speak or teach at all in the name of Jesus. But Peter and John replied, 'Which is right in God's eye: to listen to you, or to Him? You be the judges! As for us, we cannot help speaking about what we have seen and heard.' After further threats they let them go. They could not decide how to punish them, because all the people were praising God for what had happened."

Peter's attitude toward persecution strengthened the church body. On another occasion, when he was imprisoned by the Jewish political leaders, Peter and the apostles felt honored to be persecuted for Jesus. Acts 5:41 says, "The apostles left the Sanhedrin, rejoicing because they had been counted worthy of suffering disgrace for the Name."

Peter took a stand for truth, which directly opposed the political and religious systems of his day. He was later executed for advancing Christianity.

Peter was convinced that it was such a high honor to die for Jesus that he refused to die on the cross in the same manner as Jesus. Peter felt so strongly about it, he was crucified upside down. This was the same guy who denied knowing Jesus when he was first tested. Peter was an ordinary man, just a fisherman whom God used to change the world.

Dietrich Bonhoeffer is another ordinary Christian who stood against one of the most vicious and evil leaders the world has ever seen. Dietrich was a pastor and a teacher from Germany during Hitler's reign. Hitler controlled pastors, their teachings, and the entire church in countries within His reach. But Dietrich refused to comply with Hitler's demands. He continued to teach others at an underground German Bible college. He also spoke up against Hitler's atrocities of murdering an entire generation of Jews. Opposing Hitler was unheard of, especially in Germany where it was considered a death wish. Dietrich was later imprisoned, and they eventually hung him for speaking out against Hitler's mass murder of Jewish people.

Dietrich's commitment to Jesus and willingness to face death to advance Christianity still stands as an example for the entire church body to follow. His books are still published today. Read *The Cost of Discipleship* to get more insight.

Let's look at another ordinary Christian God used for extraordinary purposes. Dr. Martin Luther King Jr. also stood up against injustices for an entire race of people. He was just a pastor who put himself in the middle of our country's racial injustices during one of the most turbulent times in American history. Dr. King became a prominent leader in our country. Some Christian leaders at that time considered Dr. King to be the conscience of America, and God is the One who gave him that influence, not man. Dr. King's passion to see justice and equality launched him into the most heated racial issues our country has wrestled with for hundreds of years. His efforts were a turning point for our entire country, and he endured extreme persecution and hatred for it. The hatred came from everywhere, including the church and his own race--from the very people he stood up for.

Dr. King and his family endured frequent death threats, but it did not deter him from putting himself and his family in danger. He was imprisoned and beaten several times. In fact, he was ridiculed and slandered by religious leaders, political leaders, and other activists, very similar to Paul's treatment in the Bible. Dr. King was later murdered by a gunshot to the head.

Dr. King's dream of equality and unity is still being realized today. His commitment to God's truth continues to inspire generations. The impact of his lifelong commitment to the Great Commission is alive and well. In fact, it is still unfolding today. His life's work transcends time, and it stands as an example to our entire nation. Dr. King's legacy lives on.

One more example hits home with one of the current issues we wrestle with today. Jack Phillips is a Christian business owner in Colorado. He owned a business selling wedding cakes. His story became national news when Jack refused to sell a wedding cake to a homosexual couple in July 2012. This occurred after the government made same sex marriages legal. Jack stated that his religious beliefs would not allow him to sell a cake to the couple in support of their homosexual marriage. The customer took him to court, where the state ordered Jack to change his business practices and sell cakes for homosexual weddings. Jack refused to make a profit from something that is a sin toward God, so he shut down that part of his business. He decided to quit making wedding cakes altogether and it cost him almost half his business revenue, not to mention the backlash from media and gay activist groups. But Jack did not give up. He stuck to his biblical values.

Jack took his case to the Supreme Court, where he challenged Colorado's decision. The state's decision was overturned in June 2018. Jack fought for six years before it was overturned. His persistence paid off.

Jack's actions are a perfect example of how an ordinary person can take a stand for truth and righteousness in businesses and in our government systems. However, there was a cost for Jack to take a stand. The entire ordeal cost Jack money, time, stress, and a form of persecution. In the end, Jack trusted God to be his provider. Jack knew he was only giving up things that are temporary for the greater cause of Jesus and His ways.

His actions proved that his love for Jesus stands above everything else. Jack's actions spoke loud and clear. He was willing to lay down everything to follow Jesus. Jack's actions sent a loud message that most of our nation heard. And it encouraged other believers that anyone can do the same.

The examples above were not stories of super Christians. On the contrary, they were just ordinary people who showed extraordinary courage when faced with some of the most horrific and challenging circumstances of their day. These ordinary people were willing to sacrifice temporary comforts or die for Jesus. They took Jesus' words to heart when He said, "Take up your cross and follow me" in Matthew 16:24, and "If you love me, you will keep my commands" from John 14:15.

You can find countless others who died for the name of Jesus and the advancement of biblical Christianity, and they all have something in common. They considered death an honor, and they trusted Jesus to strengthen them during their circumstances. These

Christians possessed a different depth of love for Jesus, a deeper commitment to God's ways.

It is imperative that we intentionally study the Bible to understand Jesus' expectations for us to shine His light in the face of evil and wickedness. As you read through the New Testament, pay special attention to how the early church embraced persecution with honor and often with excitement. Many were willing to suffer poverty and hardship for the kingdom. The Bible mentions suffering and persecution a lot. The scripture in 1 Peter 4:1 shows the significance of maintaining the right attitude. "Therefore, since Christ suffered in his body, arm yourselves also with the same attitude, because whoever suffers in the body is done with sin."

Embrace it with the correct attitude and keep the correct perspective. Serving God is not a sacrifice. It is an honor. When you respond to persecution as an honor, it gives the entire church courage and builds your faith. The correct response sends a message that is loud and clear: *We can do this together because God will see us through.*

Read this powerful statement from Hebrews 11:32-38 to see how God views it:

> And what more shall I say? I do not have time to tell about Gideon, Barak, Samson and Jephthah, about David and Samuel and the prophets, who through faith conquered kingdoms, administered justice, and gained what was promised; who shut the mouths of lions, quenched the fury of the flames, and escaped the edge of the sword; whose weakness was turned to strength; and who became powerful in battle and routed foreign armies. Women received back their dead, raised to life again. There were others who were tortured, refusing to be released so that they might gain an even better resurrection. Some faced jeers and flogging, and even chains and imprisonment. They were put to death by stoning, they were sawed in two; they were killed by the sword. They went about in sheepskins and goatskins, destitute, persecuted and mistreated–the world was not worthy of them.

This scripture describes ordinary people who the world was not worthy of them. All because they took a stand and trusted in the Lord—such a powerful statement that resonates in my soul. It stirs me and encourages me to set my sights on more significant issues in our nation. I'm sure it stirs you as well.

As we ponder a new mindset and imagine the adversities we may face, keep in mind that God will not waste our hurt and pain. He uses our courageous actions of faith to change hearts, change lives and change the world. It's important to meditate on these things and allow them to resonate in our mind and sink into our heart, creating a new mindset. This life is not about us. It is about God, His plans, His church, and His kingdom. We are privileged to live and die for Jesus and His kingdom.

Begin asking the Holy Spirit to give you the courage to live out this mindset, and you will become more useful to God and His purposes. Then the Holy Spirit will begin launching you into your biggest destiny that He has purposed for your life.

You can learn more about persecution currently occurring worldwide, including the religious prisoners of today, at The Voice of The Martyrs' website @ www.Persecution.com.

I'm going to wrap up this chapter with a story about David and Goliath that mirrors our current condition. There was a moment in David's life when he watched his fellow countrymen cower in fear against the Philistine army. Fear paralyzed Israel when they faced physical threats from a giant named Goliath. However, David had a strong belief in God and his country's destiny. He valued those things deeply. David's values compelled him to put his life on the line against an enormous, trained warrior. He faced that giant head-on, for God and his people. And we all know who won the battle between David and Goliath. A battle between a seemingly weak shepherd boy and a strong, giant soldier. God had the victory on that day, and God will undoubtedly have the victory on our day.

I can almost hear David taking his stance today against the demonic force trying to destroy the American church, as David leads the charge with his most famous cry. *Is there not a time to take a stand? Is there not a truth worth living for? Is there not an injustice worth dying for?*

Where is the American church's passion and commitment to willingly embrace the honor of facing persecution and even death for the King and His kingdom?

John F. Kennedy made a powerful statement that seems fitting right now. He said, "In the long history of the world, only a few generations have been granted the role of defending freedom in the hour of maximum danger. I do not shrink back from this responsibility, I welcome it."

We are honored to live in this moment. In fact, we were born for this historic moment.

If we don't stand now, then when? If not you, then who?

5

It Starts Within

The biggest question in our mind should be, where should I start and where does my biggest destiny lie? The short answer is that it lies within us. Significant change always starts within our own hearts. This statement is so much more than just a cliché. Changing our part of this world is a God-sized task, and our relationship with Jesus holds the key. We are totally incapable of fixing the wrongs in the world on our own.

Significant change will not get accomplished through a better economy, gun control, free healthcare, or any other political hot topic. Nor will the course of our nation be changed by creating new laws, distributing stimulus money, creating better foreign policies, or ensuring Social Security benefits. Those things are only an attempt to treat the symptoms of much deeper problems. The root of our problem lies deep inside our hearts. Therefore, we must change our nation from the inside out.

The collapse of our nation can be avoided, but the change must begin within our mindsets and inside our own hearts. We need a shift in our paradigm. It is easy to see how our current mindset blurs our perspective of the rest of the world.

For example, our country is shielded and unaware of how the rest of the world lives. There are a couple of reasons I'll name. Many of us have never visited a third world country to experience firsthand true poverty. Also, our government overprotects us from many of the dangers that are commonplace in many countries. Lastly, the level of wealth of the common person in America is magnitudes higher than that of almost every other country on the planet.

Many third-world countries struggle to eat enough for survival, while we get to choose what types of food we are in the mood to eat during each meal. On top of that, most Americans possess a sense of entitlement, as if we have a God-given right to receive more for doing less. Our attitude of entitlement is perceived by other countries as if Americans think we are better than foreigners, just because we are born in the U.S. Our wealth and military power do not make us better than anyone else.

Most Americans lack exposure or never experience first-hand. Therefore, our perception of how the rest of the world lives is distorted. The wealth and power that our country possesses have shielded us from the struggle and suffering the rest of the world endures. I'm sure there are several reasons for our distorted perception, but I believe the reasons I stated above play a big part in the problem.

We are blinded to the depth of our arrogance and sense of entitlement, which means we cannot see the gravity of our own condition. Our mindset must change to allow us to see our internal problems more clearly, from God's perspective. This is only a small example to point out that we have blind spots that are blatant to the rest of the world. We have many more issues and blind spots.

While identifying the problem is a good start, healing is the goal. You cannot cure a disease by treating the symptoms. It requires deep healing down to the root. We are incapable of curing the sickness that afflicts us without the life-changing power of Jesus. Jesus is the only One in whom we can entrust our hope for a brighter future.

Healing is often a lifelong journey that begins and ends with a committed relationship of pursuing Jesus. But it will not be easy. It is one of our most difficult journeys. The old saying is true, that we are often our own worst enemies. Our biggest battle will often be fought within our own souls.

The most challenging obstacles can lie within the framework of our minds and emotions. It is the place where wars are won and lost. However, God created us to be an overcomer. This is our moment to stand against the biggest giants inside of us that have held us back— the insecurities, crippling fears, false feelings of inadequacy, lying demons from our past, or the haunting hurt and pain that shackle our soul. All the destructive things must go. Without healing, our internal issues can create a narrow mindset that limits our level of usefulness to God and His purposes. We were not created to live under the weight of these lies. When we decide to follow Jesus, there are blessings of freedom that come from God's hand.

If you haven't figured out the goal of this chapter yet, it is intended to start you on a path to find your best self and your biggest place in God's kingdom. Everything good in our lives flows from a thriving relationship with Jesus. It is the only thing that makes life worth living. Our relationship with Jesus is the only path toward fulfilling God's destiny for our lives.

This chapter contains foundational elements every Christian will need for their walk of faith. Get ready to dig in a little deeper and take plenty of notes so you can begin applying them to your life now. We're going to shift gears to talk a little about destiny. I won't go too deep, yet. I'll save that for the final chapter, after we take a journey through each facet of our culture from a biblical worldview. The journey will allow us to come full circle, with a renewed mindset and a whole new outlook.

Here we go.

At some point, you have probably had someone tell you that God has a unique purpose for your life. And I'm sure you have done your best to believe it or fulfill it. However, all too often, we don't hear more than a motivational speech about our destiny. Then we are often left to figure out the next steps on our own. There is so much more to your destiny than a motivational speech, and fortunately, it is much easier to get started than you think.

Our destiny is more of a journey than a final destination. I believe that the destiny of a Christian's life is the product of our journey through life and the decisions we make along the way. It is a road of preparation, opportunities, and faith decisions. It can also be a place of detours, roadblocks, and perceived failures.

Your journey of fulfilling God's destiny for your life involves making incrementally deeper commitments to loving Jesus and following His ways. Too often, Christians are satisfied with taking their first few steps toward serving Jesus, and they stop there.

Some people never really develop a thriving relationship with Jesus that continuously grows over time. For example, many people experience an encounter with God and get delivered from addictions, violence, depression, or other self-destructive lifestyles, and they simply stop there. They get to know Jesus, and God quickly opens doors for them, such as getting a better job, resolving a divorce, or something else they need. Once they get what they need and feel as if things are better, their commitment to Jesus quickly fizzles out.

Fortunately, there is much more to Christianity than merely keeping your personal demons at bay or keeping your head above water. When you are only doing enough to keep afloat, it can often be a miserable life. It can make you feel like you are treading water in a sea of problems, drowning within yourself.

How do you get past this point in your life? Well, it's called spiritual maturity and it is tied to our level of commitment to Jesus. There are steps toward growth and maturity. Salvation is only the first step of our life's journey toward God's plans and purposes for us. Freedom from personal issues is another important step. We will undoubtedly need courage to confront our biggest internal obstacles.

Some of us have overcome extreme circumstances that kill most people on the inside. You may have survived horrific things that could take a lifetime to heal. But it does not mean your destiny is limited. On the contrary, it usually means God can do more with our life when we garner the courage to face our biggest giants. God does His best work with the most broken and unlikely people. God will use our broken places to do the most significant things.

Freedom begins with simple steps of faith that unlock internal barriers, which are often hidden deep inside. Freedom means moving past insecurities, fears, thoughts of being inadequate, and all the other things trying to hold you down. Unfortunately, wrestling with recurring issues of personal obedience, fear, and faithlessness won't get it done. Our past experiences can often dictate how we see the world and how we respond to people or situations. More about healing later. For now, we'll simply say that a lack of healing can hold us back from walking in blind faith.

God is calling us to higher level of maturity that is capable of more than merely getting by with our same old levels of obedience and relationship with Jesus. Our life's foundation must be rooted in a growing relationship and an ever-deepening trust in the Lord. That's how God chooses to bring our faith to a place where we are willing to give Jesus whatever He asks for. We should always strive to grow in our level of obedience and faithfulness. They are the staples in our life that breed maturity. Unfortunately, possessing blind trust in God seems to be the exception rather than the norm, and we need to change that. Some believers call it radical faith, while the Bible teaches that it is plain obedience.

One of the most popular questions I receive about maturity is how to get there fast. Unfortunately, there is not a secret recipe you can use to catapult you into maturity. It takes time, coupled with consistency and resilience.

However, there is a route that will get you there the fastest. It still takes time, but you can avoid pitfalls. You can start with the right attitude. There are a couple of characteristics that hinder progress toward maturity. They deal with pride and ego. We need to always remain teachable, willing to admit our wrongdoings, and most importantly, maintain a humble outlook. There are other important things that help us avoid setbacks along the way and keep us moving forward at a steady pace.

Another critical thing that will help us mature faster is having the right people in our life. We all need mentors and spiritual fathers or spiritual mothers in our lives. A good one will help make the difference between reaching our highest calling and being most effective, or always feeling as if we are falling short of God's plans. It truly is a faster track because we learn from experienced leaders who have already traveled a path that is similar to ours. Oftentimes, they can help us reach higher than we are capable of on our own. We can grow twice as fast in half the time. Now we are still talking years of growth, but a good mentor or spiritual parent can often help us learn from their own life's achievements and mistakes.

Spiritual parenting is such a critical subject, and I'm going to cover it in more depth during a later chapter. For now, you need to know there are three things required to find and fulfill God's biggest destiny for our life, and they are: the Word of God, the Spirit of God, and the people of God.

Commit yourself to a process of being shaped and molded by God's Spirit, God's Word, and God's people. This is a lifelong process that involves an openness toward God's hand to reshape you from the inside out. Learn to be teachable, keep your pride in check, and stay humble because you do not know everything about the depths of God and His ways. You never will reach such a place. Put people in your life who know more than you and have a successful track record of guiding people. Stay faithful to the things God has you doing today. Do not look too far ahead because you may screw up the things God is doing in your life right now.

The final thing I want to share about maturity, at this point, has to do with engaging in ministry. There is no substitute that grows us more than when we serve others. We must deal with all sorts of issues that require us to get past your own opinions, feelings of being right, and we relinquish our right to fight back with revenge. Serving others produces deeper growth than merely reading a book can do. We cannot stay on the bench forever. We can only go so far by watching others do it. Some things can only be learned by doing them.

Lastly, we cannot skip steps. Otherwise, we will find ourselves in a place where our immaturity causes more damage than good.

Let's shift gears and talk about faithfulness because it builds maturity. Faithfulness is a big deal, and it deserves some detailed discussion. We will dive into some basic staples of faithfulness that will produce constant growth throughout our life.

Many things in our lives seem beyond our control. In fact, we're unable to control simple things within our own hearts. Sometimes our own actions and thoughts seem out of our control. However, there are things we can control. When we are faithful to a few important things, it will give God something to work with throughout our life's journey. Remaining faithful in good times and hard times will mature us, make us stronger, and build a stronger foundation that keeps us centered on Jesus and His ways throughout our life's ups and downs.

Here are some basic staples of faithfulness for every person who considers themselves a Christian, along with some solid suggestions to help us develop the elements of a strong foundation for the rest of our life!

1. *Read the Bible every day*. Reading daily is more than merely opening the Bible randomly and reading a chapter you happen to land on. The strength of our faith cannot hinge on reading a couple of psalms each day. Studying to write a sermon or reading books are just extra things that make us more well-rounded. But none of these things can fulfill our intimacy with Jesus. Read in a way that allows Scripture to speak into your soul.

   Here are tips that will help. Develop some sort of reading plan to get through the Bible in a year. There are several apps that contain reading plans. I personally use an app called Read Scripture. The app includes videos which provide insight into every Bible book, and they also explain how each book ties in with the rest of the Bible. If electronic reading plans are too complicated, the easiest reading plan is to start in Genesis and read three or four chapters daily until you finish Revelation. Then start all over again. If we read in that manner, the Bible will start coming to life in deeper ways. The Holy Spirit will begin helping us connect the dots of the entire Bible in ways that grow our faith, help find our identity and life's purposes, and it reveals God's expectations and promises. God's kingdom will become clearer than ever before. We will see the face of God in deeper unimaginable ways. If we continue that cycle of faithfulness for the rest of our lives, we will experience consistent maturity.

2. *Spend time alone with Jesus, praying daily.* Intimacy with Jesus is more than praying for situations throughout the day, praying while traveling to our job, or praying for our food. It goes beyond praying for friends and family. Those are good things, but we must have focused time alone with God in a place where we are not distracted. This is where our intimacy

with Jesus is established and will be launched into new depths. Nothing else can replace it and nothing else will do. Spend time with Jesus in a place you can focus, alone. Spend time worshiping, pouring out your heart, intercession, praying for your family's future, praying for your marriage, and learning to hear the voice of God. Or simply seek the heart of God and the things that grieve His heart. These are merely examples of different types of prayers. Search the Bible for different types of prayers that you can learn. It will deepen your prayer life. You will learn to hear God's voice and touch His throne during good times and life's worst times. Daily prayer increases our faith and results in continuous growth. There may be situations when we must go out of our way to get time alone daily, but there's no excuse to neglect our relationship with Jesus. Too many Christians don't know what to do or say when they are alone with Jesus for more than thirty minutes because their prayer lives might be inadequate. They only know what Jesus has done for them in a momentary encounter and they really do not know the King. Spending time alone with Jesus daily will bring His face into focus and bring clarity to God's voice. Keep this in mind. Jesus' blood provided us with direct access to God's throne. His presence is the place where we find peace, protection, direction, and renewing. Our personal prayer time, at God's throne, becomes the most holy place in our entire universe.

3. *Attend and support your local church.* Supporting the local church body is a crucial element for us to be effective on an international scale. We each have a part to play within God's global plans, and everyone must do their individual part. We can start learning how to do our part by attending services weekly, volunteering in ministries, developing deep relationships of give-and-take, and becoming an integral part of our local church family. It is not always easy to remain faithful in our local church family. We will encounter issues similar to those we deal with inside our own family. However, this is God's family and we do not have a choice to love each other and work together. In fact, we are supposed

to honor one another and serve one another. The local church is where patience and maturity are earned and learned. Once we learn how to work together with the local church, then we are better able to work together with the national or international church. Skipping steps will quickly take us to a position beyond our capabilities, where we are over our heads making mistakes and causing damage to relationships, or worse. There is more at stake than you think. Besides those things, working in God's kingdom is a privilege. We are not entitled to it, nor have we earned it.

4. *Tithing your income.* Tithing is more than merely dropping a few bucks into the bucket at church. It goes beyond giving money to the homeless guy holding a sign at the corner or sending some cash to a ministry on the internet. In fact, donating to our favorite charities does not fulfill our responsibility to tithe. Those types of giving should be done on top of tithing. The Bible teaches us to tithe a minimum of 10 percent from every dollar of our income. Consistent tithing tells God we trust Him with everything. Tithing

consistently to our local church keeps Jesus in His rightful place of ownership within the depths of our heart. It keeps idols from controlling our life or possessing an unhealthy love for power or money. Even more, it creates a deeper level of faithfulness to God throughout our lives, during times of plentiful and poor. Everything we have comes from God and we must manage it well. If we are unable to manage something as simple as tithing, how can we expect God to make us responsible for bigger things? We can learn some of our biggest lessons with tithing, such as holding onto money loosely, keeping greed from our heart, and managing money well. faithful tithing grows our obedience in other areas of our life too. Plus, we are Christians, and we are required to be generous with everything God gives us. Generosity is how God's blessings flow and how His kingdom operates. If we feel hesitant when giving, it is a sign that we have heart issues that will limit our level of usefulness to God. It is also an indication that we probably have deeper trust issues that stunt the growth of our faith. Tithing faithfully helps us become a generous giver in all areas of our life. I wholeheartedly believe that God will give us responsibilities that stretch over cities, regions, and nations if you become a generous giver and a wise steward of resources.

There's a parable in Matthew 25:23 about managing money. The verse summarizes the benefits of stewarding money in a wise and faithful manner. "His master replied, 'Well done, good and faithful servant! You have been faithful with a few things; I will put you in charge of many things. Come and share your master's happiness!'"

Here are suggestions to help if we are not consistent with the basic staples of faithfulness above. It is best for us to stop everything we are doing right now and reprioritize our entire life around these essential elements. This is especially critical if we are ministering in any capacity. Establish a consistency of faithfulness in each of the four elements. Then we can slowly add other responsibilities back into our life. Learn how to keep the important things prioritized in your everyday life before overwhelming yourself with added responsibilities.

Here are some very strong statements you should let sink into your heart:

We should not work for the King unless we are spending intimate time getting to know the King.

We should not work in God's kingdom unless we are faithfully reading to learn how to operate within His kingdom.

The kingdom is all about God and what He wants. Jesus doesn't need to use us, nor can we earn our way to the top. We cannot allow the wrong mindset to creep into our thoughts. Entitlement and payback are the wrong reasons to work for God.

Here's another reason I made these big statements about reading and praying. If we are unfaithful in our reading and praying, then we won't know if we are building God's kingdom according to His requirements. This can lead to becoming more concerned with *how* to build in God's kingdom, rather than *what* we are building within God's kingdom. There's a big difference between how we are building and what we are building. One of them gives Jesus what He wants, while the other one is more concerned with how we go about producing results. And we could be producing fruit that looks different from what Jesus requires. This speaks to disobedience in the way we lead God's kingdom. It is a different type of disobedience that is rarely discussed because we most often talk about obedience in our personal lives.

Our goal should be to continuously get stronger as we go, so we can become more useful to God. Then He can give us increasingly significant assignments, allowing us to gain momentum as we travel our destiny's path. Ending our life with a strong finish is the ultimate way to complete the race God has put in front of us.

Our life's purposes flow from the depth of our relationship with Jesus. To know Him is to know our true selves. Our identities are buried within the depths of our relationships with Jesus. As we grow in understanding and knowledge of Jesus Christ, we will begin taking on His characteristics more and more.

We are going to read a list of the Holy Spirit's characteristics in Galatians 5:22-23. "The Holy Spirit produces this kind of fruit in our lives: love, joy, peace, patience, kindness, goodness, faithfulness, gentleness, and self-control."

As you grow stronger in God's characteristics, they will begin displacing the destructive behaviors that lie within your heart. Those destructive behaviors are listed in Galatians 5:19-20, which says, "When you follow the desires of your sinful nature, the results are very clear: sexual immorality, impurity, lustful pleasures, idolatry, sorcery, hostility, quarreling, jealousy, outbursts of anger, selfish ambition, dissension, division, envy, drunkenness, wild parties and other sins like these."

Meditate on these lists and ask the Holy Spirit where you need more of Jesus and less of you.

Working in God's kingdom involves changing our personal world of influence. Real transformation in our world must start within. Internal reformation is the seed that blossoms, grows, and eventually bears fruit into our external world. Therefore, change begins within the deepest crevices of our own hearts because the condition of our heart shapes our personal values that govern our everyday actions.

The importance of growing beyond the struggles of our internal condition cannot be stressed enough. Internal struggles keep us preoccupied with an internal fight, while Satan devours our future. Our soul can only be healed and made whole by maintaining a growing relationship with Jesus. Oftentimes, our internal battles pose seemingly impossible obstacles, and they cause us to hurt others. We can be our own worst enemy. The wrong mindset or attitude can allow our mortal enemy to use our internal issues against us and keep us bound. We will discuss this topic in more detail during subsequent chapters. For now, I'll simply say, if you deal with fear, depression, distrust, insecurities, or you are a control freak, the enemy could be using them against you as a tactic. These are the types of issues that destroy relationships. We could remain unhealed until these issues are addressed. But rest assured, the Lord said in 2 Chronicles 20:17: "You will not have to fight this battle. Take up your positions; stand firm and see the deliverance the Lord will give you, Judah, and Jerusalem. Do not be afraid; do not be discouraged. Go out to face them tomorrow, and the Lord will be with you."

There is one important subject we must also review in more detail. Hearing God's voice is a critical facet of our relationship with Jesus. God is always speaking, but we are not always listening. In fact, we don't always know how to listen. Many people are a little confused about the many ways God chooses to speak to us. However, one thing is crystal clear: We must learn how to hear God's voice. If not, we will never find and fulfill God's biggest plans for our life. We will miss out on God's biggest blessings, and we will be ineffective and unproductive at kingdom building. Hearing God's voice is the most crucial element for our lives.

God's voice reveals His promises, blessings, character, and His will for our life. God's words are life-giving. His mere voice can change circumstances and situations. His voice gives us direction, hope, and strength. There is nothing like it and there is no substitute for it. Jesus went to the mountain regularly and so should we.

We do not need to be a prophet to hear God's voice. Some of us might even think we are not very prophetic at all. That is far from the truth. Every Christian is prophetic at some level, by the very nature of who we are. We all hear from God in different ways. In fact, every Christian is an ambassador for Jesus, and we have the honor of speaking to others on God's behalf. But it takes time and effort to hear God's voice in every circumstance. A consistent prayer life is a key to hearing God during life's hardest times. Sometimes we need persistence to hear God's voice. It's not always easy. There are even times when we cannot seem to hear from God at all.

Every Christian has probably experienced some sort of spiritual block, where we cannot seem to get through to hear God. It doesn't mean we should give up. On the contrary, we need to do the opposite. We must become more determined to hear Him by frequently seeking Jesus, reading God's Word, and receiving guidance from a spiritual leader.

God speaks in many ways. In some ways, God's words are black and white, and in other ways that He speaks, it can seem difficult to discern. Sometimes it can be difficult to determine whether the voice we are hearing is coming from God, our own mind, other people's words ringing through our head, or demons putting thoughts into our mind. In those cases, we need to dig into our Bible to sort things out, remain still, and wait on the Lord.

Here is a list of ways God speaks. They are arranged from the most reliable and easiest to hear, to the more difficult to understand.

1. **Bible** – This is the most reliable and sure way to *hear* God. It is black and white, but it takes careful study to fully understand. We will spend our lifetime uncovering the endless depths of its truths.

2. **Prayer and voice of the Spirit** – This could be an audible voice, or you might sense His voice in your soul. He might impress something upon your heart or mind, etc. It mostly happens during your quiet time with God. It is one of the reasons that consistent quiet time is crucial.

3. **Dreams and visions** – Dreams are projected onto our mind, like a movie on a projector screen. Visions are seen in the mind's eye or literally seen. They may involve symbolism, which requires interpretation. This type of communication can take years of committed study to become proficient in. Guidance from someone experienced can be essential. Use your Bible to interpret the symbols and words. Ask the Holy Spirit to fill in the gaps. This is often a reliable way for God to communicate with us. But again, we must spend time

studying to accurately interpret dreams and visions, especially if this is the major way God speaks to you.

4. **Church body** – Other Christians also hear God's voice, and then they speak to us on His behalf. Many times, it confirms what God has already been saying to us. Other times, it gives us direction that might take years to fully unfold. Prophetic words can take many years to be fulfilled in our life. Nonetheless, guidance from prophetic words must align with the Bible. A good piece of advice is to seek guidance from people who love us and care deeply for us.

5. **Circumstances** – These are usually seen as coincidences or situations that speak to us in a specific way that typically confirms God's voice or His will. This source of communication is usually the least reliable because it is usually the most difficult to interpret. There are rare occasions when we may receive hundreds of repeated circumstances, and those are easier to discern. As a rule of thumb, it is best to avoid making big life-changing decisions that are solely based upon circumstances, but there can be

exceptions to that rule. Regardless, we need an encounter with God for guidance on our destiny, not a sign. Keep pressing into God if you are unable to hear anything from Him on important life decisions. Lean on His Word, spend lots of time in prayer, and get guidance from a spiritual parent. We may need to stand still awhile. Keep in mind that God does not force us into the path of His will. He usually urges us within our heart, and He opens doors of opportunity. Unfortunately, we may not hear from God in a clear and definitive way when He is making big changes in our life. We many only receive coincidences, minimal revelation from friends or other believers and an impression on our heart. God usually uses His quietest voice to ask us to take our biggest steps of faith.

Do you want to learn more about hearing the voice of God? Read the book by Cindy Jacobs called *The Voice of God: How to Hear and Speak Words from God*. Your communication with God will improve dramatically.

The more we seek God's voice, the more we will grow to know Him in deeper ways. I will let you in on a little secret. We will never know the fullness of who God is—not in this lifetime. We will never arrive at a place where we know everything about God or His ways. We will not become some sort of super Christian who knows God better than everyone else. It just doesn't work like that.

Our relationship with Jesus cannot be taken lightly. It must be our number one priority throughout our entire life. Do not think of our relationship with God as a balancing act. We do not balance it with the rest of our life's activities. How can we balance God? We must make time for God every day. Everything we cherish most in our life flows from our relationship with Jesus, including our future. Conversely, everything will fall apart if we overlook it.

The moment when we think we know Him the deepest is when something usually happens that turns our world upside down. Difficult situations and personal tragedy can make us realize how little we really know Him. Tragedy has a way of shaking up our faith and making us realize how weak we are without Jesus. In other words, we do not know God as well as we think we do, and our faith and love for Jesus are always much weaker than we realize. It is the reality Peter got slapped in the face with when he told Jesus that he would go to prison and die for Him in Luke 22:33.

Peter thought he loved Jesus more than anybody else. He probably felt like he had a right to think that way. Just look at Peter's life up to that moment. He is the only person on the planet to walk on water with Jesus. He even saw Jesus transfigured. He saw a face of Jesus that very few people on the planet have ever seen. If anyone had the right to brag, it should have been Peter.

Unfortunately, when Peter's world got super rough, he disowned Jesus. After Jesus was captured, the Jewish religious leaders were treating Him like a murderer. All the while, Peter denied knowing Jesus three times without a single hesitation. To make things worse, Peter denied knowing Jesus the third time with deep passion and vigor.

Thank God for the blood of Jesus. I'm sure each of us can remember our own Peter moments when we totally messed up and needed God's grace. Lord, keep us humble.

Just accept the fact that we may never begin to scratch the surface of God's magnificence and eternal majesty. He is beyond our understanding, and we are incapable of comprehending the infinite nature of God. We are merely His creations, and I am unable to fathom why He chooses to let us operate in His kingdom. All I know is, He is a big God, and it is our life's purpose to chase Him with all our strength.

So how important is hearing God's voice? His voice is life, and within it lies our most significant destiny. At different moments in our lives, hearing God's voice can mean life or death.

There is much more that could be said about how the fundamentals described in this chapter contribute to our personal growth and maturity. However, the things we covered will provide a strong foundation that we will spend the rest of our life building. There is one more thing I would feel negligent about if I failed to emphasize the importance of it. Come to grips with the fact that we will only get as much out of our own maturity and relationship with Jesus as we put into it. The more diligent and dedicated we become, the bigger outcome we will see.

From this moment forward, ask the Lord to reveal the things He wants to transform within you and remove from your heart. Seek the Holy Spirit for courage to face your deepest places head on, asking that He will provide blind faith that trusts in what He is doing and the places He is taking you.

6

Family First

You have probably heard it said that ministry starts at home. The truth is that our responsibilities for our families go deeper than we realize, and it's not an easy task. In fact, the relationships inside our homes are usually the most challenging thing we will ever do, but they are also the most important for the future of Christianity. My perspective on our responsibilities to our families is that if we fail at being a godly spouse and parent, then we have failed as Christians at our most fundamental purposes of God.

God created the institution of family during the very beginning of creation. He established the ideal of family when He commanded Adam to fill the earth and multiply in Genesis 1. Creating mankind was the crown jewel of all God's creations in our universe. And the family unit holds His most precious jewel—humankind. Establishing the family unit was the culmination of His most important creation. If God is the foundation of our world, family is the infrastructure upon which our world can be built. Without it, our world collapses. But when families function within the commands of God, His blessings flow like water.

Maintaining a godly family is the key for fulfilling our most important historical achievements. Satan has attacked family relationships from the very beginning of time when Adam and Eve were in the garden of Eden. Eve convinced her husband to sin against God and Adam decided to go along with it. He was the leader, and he made a decision to lead his family astray. It should have never happened on his watch.

After God confronted Adam, instead of repenting, Adam blamed both his wife and God for his transgressions. "The man said, 'The woman you put here with me – she gave me some fruit from the tree, and I ate it'" (Genesis 3:13).

This was Satan's first time dividing a marriage and turning a family away from God. Since that day, the devil has been turning families away from God, and he has become a master at it.

Today, families across the world are under extreme levels of destruction in unimaginable ways. Satan's tactics have reached new depths of wickedness. He continuously creates new ways to destroy families and rip them away from God and God's blessings. Satan and his demons have pulled out all the stops to decimate families and their futures. He has taken his tactics to new levels of intensity. He is targeting fathers, mothers, sons, and daughters. The devil is even targeting the reproductive nature of all mankind through the prolific growth of same sex marriages.

There is an all-out war to corrupt every father, crush the soul of every mother, kill every child, and destroy the sacred institution of marriage. When you think about the things happening in our world today, Satan's strategies become clearer. His goal is to decimate every family and crush the very ideal of family to remove it from the inherent values of our culture.

Look at the issues plaguing our world and think about how it destroys our fathers, sons, mothers, and daughters. We are dealing with destructive and horrific issues from sex trafficking, addictions, rape, abortions, and a whole slew of unimaginable sin and wickedness. Satan's tactics crush the soul, kill the spirit, and try to remove God's sacred institution of marriage from the face of the earth.

Fatherlessness, where children grow up without a father for any number of reasons, is a chronic and tragic problem. God's most precious crown jewel and the setting that holds it together are being broken beyond recognition. Broken marriages produce broken children. Broken children become dysfunctional adults. Dysfunctional adults produce dysfunctional families. Those families reproduce children that fall into the same cursed life, and their lifestyle usually gets worse every generation.

Exodus 20:5 says, "You shall not bow down to them or worship them; for I, the Lord your God, am a jealous God, punishing the children for the sin of the parents to the third and fourth generations of those who hate me."

This vicious cycle has already spiraled out of control. These cycles in our culture are started at home within our families. Healthy families are the foundation of a healthy society, as opposed to broken and dysfunctional families, which typically create broken children. Dysfunctional families make the children feel as if they are inadequate, which often creates issues, such as feelings of or actual abandonment or rejection.

The most prevalent cause of these issues, and many more, is children growing up without a father. In fact, fatherlessness does not always mean the absence of a father. It can also mean the absence of a father's love in a child's life, regardless of whether he is present in his or her childhood. Here is what I mean: Some fathers cause more damage by being present than if they were absent from a child's life altogether.

Fatherlessness is breaking our culture. Broken cultures are self-centered and self-serving, and they victimize others. There is a cost to these types of cultures. They create a mindset to protect themselves and rely on their own strength to get what they want. Self-centered cultures eventually remove God's commands, values, and blessings. Broken cultures create cycles that continue reproducing people whose lifestyle gets worse with each generational cycle, unless they turn to Jesus and follow His ways.

Satan is creating a pandemic of fatherlessness one family at a time. It has now become acceptable in our culture to have children out of wedlock, while divorce and same sex marriage are largely considered acceptable. Meanwhile, child abuse, abandonment, and molestation are on the rise.

An evil is lurking inside of men that is killing the hearts of our families. It is causing fathers to be manipulated by the devil's hand. In turn, fatherlessness is creating wounds inside of children everywhere. It can destroy a child's future before their life begins. Some fathers who are present in their children's lives cause more damage than if they were never around. While the lack of godly fathers inflicts more damage to children than COVID-19 could ever do.

The ever-changing culture in America also contributes to the destruction of God's definition of a family. As we all know, our culture always seems to be changing over time. A culture changes with each new generation, just as our family values change from one generation to the next. Some changes have been good, and some have been very bad. As a nation, our culture has departed from

God's ways over time, one step at a time. This has caused our nation as a whole to drift away from God and His ways. If left untreated, this trajectory can only result in cursed lives for families and individuals.

On the other hand, we will receive an entirely different outcome when we follow God's commands. We will create a new cycle that keeps getting better over time. God's ways create a blessed way of life and generational blessings. A corrupt culture can only be cured with the blood of Jesus. Unfortunately, most situations typically require God's discipline before people will turn to Jesus.

Our mindset about the priority of our families must be recalibrated before we ruin our nation's future. Nothing except God is more important than our family. There are seasons or periods of time when ministry or work will occupy a significant amount of time. But we are only talking weeks or a couple of months. Nothing should keep us from being present as a parent or spouse on a consistent basis. Who will love your wife or husband if you don't? Who will raise your children if you don't? Who will lead your family if you don't? One thing is certain—Satan has figured out a way to fill the gaps.

How can we each do our part to start changing these things? Well, we begin with a growing commitment to Jesus and following His ways as a parent and spouse. Our goal should be to lead our families well, according to God's expectations. Love your wife, respect your husband, and setting a godly example of faithfulness by serving each other's needs. Spend quality time with your spouse. Invest in your children with quality time expression of love.

If we make every effort to grow as a Christian, we will see our family's desire to follow our lead. We lead our family on our knees because we need God's Spirit to lead and guide us, as parents. Leading our family by example, learning, and correcting as we go. It is the best way to lead a family.

Imagine if we had a nation full of families that raise children who are whole and healthy on the inside. We would have adults devoid of scars and trauma from their childhoods. It would be a new beginning where children are raised in homes with husbands and wives who know how to love each other and their children. Fathers and mothers who love God with their actions and follow God's ways with all their strength would create a very different world. We would have a place filled with hope and God-fueled dreams.

A key to maintaining a marriage that remains fresh, healthy, and loving is following God's ways. Families remain healthy when they are God-loving. A healthy family is the key ingredient to establishing a foundation on which our nation can build a bright new future.

There is a reason our family relationships are so difficult. Satan has put a target on every family. An invisible war is going on all around us, and the spoils of this war are our children's futures. We cannot afford to make big mistakes in this war. The future of our families is hanging in the balance, and our only option is to get it right.

The Bible is explicit about being a godly spouse and teaching our children God's ways. The responsibility of parenthood falls directly on the parents' shoulders. God will hold us accountable for teaching our children to follow Jesus, not our local church or our school system. We will create generational blessings when we invest God's ways into our children.

Joel 1:3 says, "Tell it to your children, and let your children tell it to their children, and their children to the next generation." When we combine this verse with Exodus 20:6. "But showing love to a thousand generations of those who love me and keep my commandments," you can plainly see God's promise for generational blessings. Essentially, we are inserting God's ways into our family heritage, forever changing the trajectory of our family lineage. That's how we create an eternal legacy. It may be our most significant contribution to the future of our nation and God's kingdom.

There are other ways we can help our children know the goodness of God. Share with your children the reasons why you love Jesus and all the miraculous things He has done for you. Deuteronomy 6:20-25 says,

> In the future, when your son asks you, "What is the meaning of the stipulations, decrees and laws the Lord our God has commanded you?" tell him: "We were slaves of Pharaoh in Egypt, but the Lord brought us out of Egypt with a mighty hand. Before our eyes the Lord sent signs and wonders. . . . The Lord commanded us to obey all these decrees and to fear the Lord our God, so that we might always prosper and be kept alive, as is the case today. And if we are careful to obey all this

law before the Lord our God, as He has commanded us, that will be our righteousness."

If you are a single man or woman, you may think this entire chapter will only help you in the future. On the contrary, we can turnaround a generational cycle, if we are willing to prepare ourselves now. We can start working on leading our future family before we get married or have children. For example, start following God's expectations by working on becoming a good son or daughter. Work on the things that cause broken homes, so you don't make those mistakes.

If you are looking for a new relationship, stop. Quit looking for a relationship. Learn to love Jesus before you venture into another failed relationship.

Men, learn to be good husbands and fathers now. The fact is, we will never learn to love a woman until we learn to love Jesus with our life. Then we can start looking for a wife who loves Jesus more than she will ever love us.

Be sincere to that woman when you are dating. Practice loving her with your actions by doing more than maintaining your own purity. Let your actions and intentions protect her—emotionally, physically, and spiritually. Maintain her purity. Treat her in ways that keep her integrity intact. Do not mislead her or harm her and keep temptation from her mind. Use your current relationship as an opportunity to treat her like a godly wife should be treated. Focus your efforts on becoming a godly husband and leader. Quit thinking of your own needs and start putting her needs ahead of your own.

If you are dealing with lust, pornography, or anger, address them before you get into a relationship. You may think they are small issues that won't hurt anyone else, but you are dead wrong. Seemingly small problems become amplified the moment we get married. Even issues that seem harmless can lead us to adultery or domestic violence. Each of these problems will crush a woman's soul and forever change her frame of mind.

Let's talk more about spending quality time with our family. Specifically, we will discuss our work-family balance because it is such a big issue in America. Our society has a chronic problem that is unique to our country. I can't think of another country in the world that strives so hard for success and wealth. It causes us to sacrifice the relationships of our marriages and the futures of our children.

The Unites States has become a place where wealth, success, and achieving goals outweighs our God-given command to raise healthy and whole families. We have become so busy that it has distorted our definition of success and wealth. This deception has caused us to lose sight of our most critical responsibilities, which are our families.

The busyness of our lives seems to weigh on us before we wake up, and its constant pressure keeps our mind spinning into the late hours of the night. We often feel like we are behind schedule the moment we open our eyes in the morning before the day even starts. It creates unnecessary stress that causes us to overly focus on our self-inflicted busy lives. All the while, we are missing the target.

We are not supposed to balance our marriage and family with the rest of our life's responsibilities. It is something we should prioritize and dedicate the best parts of ourselves to, not our leftovers. Our spouses and children do not need wealth or success, just our time. They need us to build and maintain meaningful relationships within our homes.

Don't be fooled into thinking your hard work outside the home somehow benefits your spouse and children's relationship with God.

Hard work or material possessions do not play into the equation of being a good father or mother. If our lives are centered on work or achieving personal goals, our lives' priorities need to be reorganized. It is easy to figure out where our actual priorities lie.

We spend the most time on the things we value the most. Here is a little exercise to help you see where your values lie. Create a small journal for two weeks. Write down where you spend your time throughout each day. After two weeks, review your journal. Your journal will reveal your true priorities. Use this information to position your family back where they belong, as the highest priority in your life.

Become intentional about meeting your God-given responsibilities. Do not rely on schools, churches, or conferences to raise and strengthen your family. Remove things that take away from your family responsibilities. Be willing to put down your own dreams for the success of your marriage and family. It's that simple and it is that important. Each of us is accountable to God for being a successful father, mother, husband, and wife.

Although we cannot control everything within our family's future, there is no excuse for failing to prioritize our own family. Raising our family to love Jesus is one of our highest callings. Lead your family into deeper places of God. Strive to create an ever-growing desire to love Jesus. Instill values within your children they can take with them to lead their own families. Lead by example and live your life in a way that leaves a legacy of Jesus worshippers. That is the type of legacy that will never die, a legacy that continues living and growing long after we are gone. That type of legacy will break generational curses forever.

Our most significant gift to the world should be the family legacy we leave behind. When our life is over and we are breathing our last breaths of life, we will not think about our achievements, success, or wealth. We will remember the memories of successes and failures of our family relationships throughout our life.

Live your life today to rewrite the script of memories you will see at your life's end. There is still time. And if you have broken relationships, God can reconcile them. He can put together the pieces of brokenness, no matter how they were broken. Take on an attitude that refuses to allow your personal achievements to mask your deceptions of *providing for your family*. Your family needs you now, and nothing less will do.

Here is a saying I personally use often: *True wealth is something money cannot buy and death can't take away.*

I don't remember where I heard it from, but it helps me keep the eternal wealth of my family in the forefront of my life.

Also keep this saying in mind. *The decisions you make today determine the legacy you will leave tomorrow.* Where does your wealth lie?

7

Revealing Our Hearts

In this chapter we will explore the heart of mankind and uncover how dark it can become when we fall too far from God's ways. To do this, we will briefly visit some of the most heinous transgressions against humanity in history. At the same time, we will examine how God can use our simple acts of faith to literally save lives during dire situations. Hopefully, this chapter will reveal two things. First, we will expose Satan's diabolic plans to destroy mankind. Then, we will show how God can use any of us to oppose Satan's plans and change the most significant issues in our culture, because nothing is too hard for God if we are willing to take a stand.

As human beings, we are capable of beautiful acts of love toward others, while at other times we are also capable of heinous crimes against humanity. For example, the United States has come to the aid of countless countries who were in dire situations. At the same time, our country has committed crimes of slavery against an entire race of people that lasted hundreds of years. How can the same nation be a global humanitarian, and that same nation also committed crimes against humanity? It is the dichotomy of our hearts' condition when we lack the love of Jesus Christ.

We will take a broader look at some history to show the extent of evil lurking inside of all mankind—a deep evil that creates wars, death, and destruction. This evil has plagued the history of mankind. The effects are all around us, and it all began the moment Adam sinned in the garden of Eden. Although we already reviewed the Dominion Mandate and the Great Commission, they are worth summarizing for the sake of this chapter, which is a turning point in this book.

In Genesis 1, God gave Adam a mandate to fill the earth, subdue it, and rule over it. At that moment, He gave Adam a tremendous amount of authority on earth. God made Adam responsible for the earth and everything in it. The first mistake Adam made with his God-given authority was to allow sin into our world. Adam granted

Satan power in this world by succumbing to his deceptive lies. Adam gave Satan a seat of authority in our world, which allowed him to use his evil intentions on everybody.

Fortunately, Jesus revoked Satan's authority with His sacrifice on the cross. Look at Jesus' words in John 12:31-32: "Now is the time for judgment on this world; now the prince of this world will be driven out. And I, when I am lifted up from the earth, will draw all people to myself."

I said all of that to say, Satan's intentions are evil all the time, and there's a method to his madness. His goal is to destroy every person on earth, and it becomes apparent when you observe how quickly Satan destroyed Adam's relationship with God. Ultimately, he corrupted Adam's family.

Adam's sin created a pandemic that quickly spread like wildfire within the hearts of every generation. To put it bluntly, his sin created an incurable cancer that is rotting us out, a cancer that can only be cured with the blood of Jesus.

Nonetheless, we still possess authority today that God granted Adam. It is an authority that transcends time and generations. I'll call it transcendent authority, a truth that is the most essential truth in this book. In fact, it's the foundational truth this book is based upon because it represents God's command that is meant to propel us into our most significant destiny, a divine destiny capable of changing the course of our world.

Suffice it to say, we need to dig a little deeper into this truth of transcendent authority. Our God-given authority allows mankind to accomplish many things, such as establishing entire countries, creating kingdoms, or generating global wealth. We can even create generations of blessed families, or we can pass along cursed and wicked ways. Sometimes we create good things and sometimes we create bad things that hurt other people. Our personal values dictate whether the things we create are blessed or cursed. The reason our values are important is because they determine our intentions, which drives our actions. Our personal values also dictate how we treat people or what we are willing to do for the things we desire.

Looking at it from a broader perspective, the personal values of the people of a nation collectively create a system of values for that nation. Value systems have created both good and bad things in our own country and other nations throughout history. Some nations have done good things, like helping other countries fight off their enemies in two world wars, sending aid to other countries to help their people at a time of natural or manmade disaster, sending missionaries around the world, and many other life-saving acts. Unfortunately, value systems can become distorted. They made destructive things acceptable, such things as racism, slavery, world wars, and even a Holocaust for an entire race of Jewish people.

We have the authority to create good, bad, and extreme evil. But there are consequences to the things our values create. The big question is, what will we continue creating? Will we create blessings or curses; prosperity or famine; peace or war; life or death?

We certainly have a choice whether we succumb to the right desires. In Genesis 4:7, the Lord talks to Cain right before he killed his brother, Abel. The Lord said, "If you do what is right, will you not be accepted? But if you do not do what is right, sin is crouching at your door; it desires to have you, but you must rule over it."

Satan certainly understands our God-given authority, and he uses it to manipulate us like puppets. He manipulates us into doing his bidding. Satan typically creates some type of void, pain or hurt inside of us that he can later use against us. Then he uses his army of fallen angels to influence our actions by manipulating our mind and emotions from our place of pain, hurt, insecurity, etc. Satan is thereby able to create a culture that will reflect his evil characteristics. In short, Satan created a way to manipulate mankind to destroy everything God loves.

You would think we should be able to see it coming and somehow avoid such manipulation. But the influence from Satan's army of fallen angels is a gradual process with strategic results. Satan's demons do his bidding by creating voids within our hearts, and they try to fill it with darkness. Pain, rejection, abandonment, and other heartbreaks create fertile ground for evil seeds to take root. Those are the places demons use against us through manipulation, just like a puppet master does. They plant thoughts into our minds and play with our emotions to get the reactions they seek, thereby creating further darkness deep inside us.

They manipulate our darkest places to create wicked and evil things, influencing us to do their will and execute their plans. It's a masterful journey of destruction, while they patiently control the outcome. We are rarely aware of the destination that our own decisions are taking us. The steps along the path are so subtle and unassuming. Many times, our lives arrive at a place we're unhappy with, and we don't even know how we got there. Our lives change and get worse by taking a bunch of tiny steps that slowly cause us to deviate from God's ways. All those tiny missteps add up to a huge departure from God's plans over the course of years and decades.

Demons are waging a war on the souls of every man, woman, and child. Their tactics are wicked and ruthless. Our mortal enemy is always on the prowl, looking to devour and destroy. He and his evil fallen angels are always watching, always listening, and always waiting—influencing us at every turn, inventing new opportunities to hurt us and break us. They never sleep, and they never stop. Satan's plans are diabolical—pure evil.

We will review a few examples that happened around the world. They should provide insight into the heart of mankind. The intent is to merely show how we got here. Keep in mind, it is not meant to paint a grim picture of hopelessness. On the contrary, we need to shed the light of God's truth on wickedness so His truth will change people's hearts, revealing how God can take our simple acts of faith to change our world.

The English language fails me when searching for words to describe the heinous crimes against humanity that we see today. Harvesting human organs and selling them to desperate Americans with money. Sex trafficking little boys and girls and forcing people to smuggle drugs across international borders are just a few things we often hear about. Not to mention the issue of abortion, the horrors of which have been stated many times in this book. This is not for the sake of being repetitive. Abortion effects people in countless ways, and I am merely trying to create awareness about the totality of its effects. Hopefully, it stirs every person who reads this book into action.

In case you didn't know, abortion is not a new issue. The Bible speaks of abortion back in the days of Moses. Although we are responsible for our own actions, make sure you acknowledge who is behind it. It's Satan and his army behind this diabolical wickedness. He has been murdering and sacrificing babies for thousands of years.

He did it twice in the Bible on mass levels. Once when Moses was born, and another time when Jesus was born. Satan is always trying to stop God's plans. He has a history of killing children when God has plans to liberate people from bondage. Here are a few examples.

In Exodus 1:15-22, Satan tried to kill Moses several times when he was born. First, he used the Pharaoh over Egypt to command the midwives to kill all newborn Israelite boys. The midwives refused and Pharaoh's first attempt failed. Then Pharaoh ordered the Egyptian citizens to throw every newborn Hebrew boy into the Nile River, drowning each newborn boy. This unimaginable edict to murder babies comes from Exodus 1:22, "Then Pharaoh commanded all his people to throw into the Nile every Hebrew boy that was born, but let every girl live."

The mass murder of Israel's baby boys must have been a horrific ordeal for parents to endure. But God turned the tables on Satan. As a newborn Israelite, Moses was supposed to be killed but he ended up being raised in Pharaoh's own palace. Satan failed to stop God's plans, and God later used Moses to deliver His people from Egyptian bondage.

Later on, Satan tried to foil God's plans again. He tried to kill Jesus after He was born. This time through King Herod. Matthew 2:16 tell us, "[Herod] gave orders to kill all the boys in Bethlehem and its vicinity who were two years old and under, in accordance with the time he had learned [about Jesus' birth]. . . ." It was another horrific moment in Israel's history. Matthew 2:18 describes how it caused "weeping and great mourning, Rachel weeping for her children and refusing to be comforted, because they are no more."

Satan once again tried to keep God from freeing His people. But God turned the tables on him once again. The death of Jesus put the final nail in Satan's own coffin.

The Bible also speaks about Israel sacrificing children to the Ammonite demonic god named Molech. Children were sacrificed by putting them in fire and burning them to death. In fact, the Bible records some wicked Israelite kings who intentionally sacrificed their own children. Second Kings 16:3 says, "He [king Ahaz] followed the ways of the kings of Israel and even sacrificed his son in the fire, engaging in the detestable practices of the nations. . . ."

Today abortion is the single most devastating act of genocide the world has ever seen. It has spilled more blood than any war during the entire history of mankind. The number of unborn children murdered is astronomical. It seems unimaginable that mankind is capable of being manipulated by demons to carry out such things for so long.

God knows that the heart of mankind is only evil all the time. Look at Genesis 6:5-7 before God flooded the earth. You'll see insight into God's thoughts about the world's corruption and violence. "The Lord saw how great the wickedness of the human race had become on the earth, and that every inclination of the thoughts of the human heart was only evil all the time. The Lord regretted that he had made human beings on the earth, and his heart was deeply troubled. So the Lord said, 'I will wipe from the face of the earth the human race I have created.'"

It's the heart of man that's at the root of our world's condition. If we will allow Jesus to change the deepest places of our hearts, we will change our world.

Here's a real story to show an example how abortion has affected our cities. There was a doctor in South Bend, Indiana, who was an abortionist. He died in September 2019. Immediately following his death, his family made a gruesome discovery. They found the remains of over 2,200 aborted babies in his house. The babies were medically preserved in jars and stored in his garage. Indiana's Attorney General gave this case special attention and arranged to give the babies a proper burial.

What was the abortionist thinking? Impossible to imagine. He took all that time to put each baby in a jar to preserve them. Raw wickedness. This man's acts were deranged and twisted in unimaginable ways. Imagine how the parents, local families and the entire city were affected by this gruesome discovery of death. His family was left in shock and was unable to properly mourn his death. In fact, the entire city felt the pain and shame of his sin.

The story goes on to discuss how old the babies would be at the time of discovery. The babies would be teenagers, starting college, exploring careers, and perhaps starting their own families. Absolutely horrifying and disgusting. Unfortunately, there are over

63 million stories of hurt and pain, in every city and within every family.

Is the demonic power of Molech behind the abortions, similar to the stories in the Bible? I would say, yes. It seems undeniable in my mind. In fact, I would go as far as saying that I believe Satan is currently trying to stop God's plans again. I believe that God has plans for His biggest harvest ever, a global move of God beyond anything we could dream of. Consequently, Satan is now trying to kill an entire generation that has been called to carry Jesus' plans of deliverance for the entire world.

I just made a huge statement that may seem delusional to some of you. I am going to make some additional comparisons to substantiate my statement. We will compare today's act of genocide with a few more of Satan's historical attempts to kill an entire generation. However, before we visit some of these events in recent history, it's important to keep the goal in mind. I am not trying to paint a grim picture of hopelessness. My goal is to create awareness of God's plans to liberate all mankind. I also want to create awareness and shed light on the enemy's plans.

119

Let's go back to Hitler's plans to eradicate every Jewish person within German reach, which resulted in an estimated nine million Jews being murdered. He engineered the most systematic and efficient machines of death the world had seen.

Slavery is another chronic issue. I am not merely talking about slavery in America. It was a global business that ripped apart families and dehumanized an entire race of people.

Today we still have a global issue with slavery, only it is much broader. We call it human trafficking. Human trafficking seems very similar to slavery in a chilling way, where humans were sold like cattle, horses, and common farm animals. Slavery was a terrible and evil part of American history. It created a civil war and its effects have remained the most heated controversy of our time.

Although similar, human trafficking has no barriers of race, color, age, or gender. It includes unimaginable things, like kidnapping people from third world countries to harvest their organs, selling people for slave labor, and creating global prostitution and pornography rings made up of women, young girls, and little boys. Human trafficking even involves twisted satanic rituals that sacrifice and cannibalize children, not to mention stealing babies from their mothers and selling them for adoption.

Are we repeating history on a bigger scale? Have we forgotten how evil slavery was? Has our nation come full circle? But this time it's not just slavery. This time, it's not just an African race. Human trafficking is blind to color, gender, and age. A new form of an old evil has been invented that is consuming everything and everybody it can. It ravages people who are unable to fight back, have no voice, destitute, and those who are unnoticed and unwanted. No nation is safe from its reach.

Go listen to the recordings of former slaves and Holocaust survivors telling their stories. There is nothing that compares to hearing the effects straight from the victims' mouths. You can find them on the Library of Congress website at www.LOC.gov and Youtube. Take a moment to watch the numerous videos of former slaves and Holocaust survivors telling their stories that have been uploaded on YouTube. Search *slave interviews audio* and *holocaust survivor interviews* on YouTube. Navigating on www.LOC.gov is more difficult because the website contains thousands of pages, but

121

YouTube is easier to navigate. Either way, the recordings put a face and a voice to the stories you have only read about. It becomes a bone chilling reality when you hear the atrocities firsthand from former slaves and Holocaust survivors. I found two things the most disturbing in the videos and recordings. Slavery created a dehumanized mindset with the interviewed slaves. Secondly, the Germans were so cold-hearted toward the Jews in the extermination camps.

Now, we will shift back to the atrocities of abortion that have occurred in our country. I believe that God has heard the cries from the blood-soaked stains on our own soil. The cries from generations of aborted children have reached His throne, and those cries have catapulted His plans into motion.

Having said that, I want to take a moment to get one thing clear. I am not condemning women who have been through an abortion. Jesus has not condemned them, and neither am I. On the contrary, I want to see those women healed, healthy and whole. We will discuss the effects of abortion on women in more detail in the next chapter. I have dedicated an entire chapter on healing our women because it is one of my life's missions. For now, we will keep focused on the things happening in our culture today. Abortion is only one example of something our culture deems acceptable, while the Bible calls it a sin. My point here is that we, as a nation, are calling bad things good, and we are calling good things bad.

If this stirs you the way it stirs me, maybe God wants you to be part of His plans to do something about it. Perhaps we can be a voice for the voiceless. Or get involved with our local or national organizations to help abolish such things. We can help heal the broken souls in the fathers and mothers, one parent at a time. That is how God's kingdom is built—one person at a time. Our simple act of love and compassion may lead to healing in thousands of hurting souls who desperately need Jesus and His healing hand.

Some of us feel as if there is nothing we can do to help. Keep this in mind, if we love Jesus, we carry His Spirit inside of us. God's divine power lives within us. The power of God's mere words catapulted our universe into existence. If He gives us the will, He will provide the way. Many times, our passion for a cause comes from the Lord.

I'd like to give you an example of a dear friend of ours whose simple act of compassion and courage saved the lives of several babies. It is a personal example to show how each of us can do our part.

My wife teaches an online Bible study with dozens of wonderful women from all over the country. Many of them have endured so many unspeakable tragedies in their lives, and God is doing such amazing things to heal them and turn their lives around. They are becoming emerging leaders in their communities, families, and God's kingdom.

During one of my wife's meetings, she asked me to speak to her group about abortion during Abortion Recovery Awareness Month. My wife knows that I am passionate about abortion and its effects on women. During my meeting with the group of women, I said a few things about abortion rates and its effects on women to make everyone aware. At the end of my talk, I challenged the group of women to ask God to show them how they could get involved in some way during that month.

I later followed up with my wife, eagerly waiting to hear what the ladies did that month to get involved. One of our dear friends, Connie, told us something that deeply moved me. Connie took the challenge to heart in an unexpected way. She began asking the Holy Spirit to give her an opportunity to help in some way. Although Connie had no idea how she could help with abortion, the Lord spoke to her about finding a local abortion clinic. She found out there was an abortion clinic a short distance from her home. One day, Connie decided to head over to the clinic and pray, so she grabbed her kids and hopped in the car. When she arrived, there was a long line that extended down the block. Connie felt the Holy Spirit tell her to pray for these women in line. She simply asked a few of the ladies in line if she could pray for them.

Connie began praying with some of the women, and suddenly God's Spirit touched those ladies. Each of the ladies began weeping. Some of the women opened up and admitted the guilt they were feeling while waiting in that line. I believe they were feeling more than sorrow and shame. Those women heard the voice of God through Connie's prayers. They felt the love and presence of Jesus.

I was ecstatic to hear that several women decided against abortion, and they left the line. Connie didn't know those women she prayed with, nor has she seen them since that day. But we do know one thing—those babies' lives were saved by God's grace that day. The babies experienced the grace of God because their mothers experienced the love of God.

On that day, God chose to send a Jesus-loving housewife to that abortion clinic to pray for those women. The Lord saved those women from a lifetime of soul-crushing pain and regret from aborting their babies. Several lives were saved that day and the Lord gave new hope to the mothers and their babies. Jesus gave them a new chance for a new future.

I often wonder how God will use those babies in His kingdom. Why did He choose to send Connie to that specific clinic on that particular day? What are His special plans for those children's futures? Will they be prophets or our next president? Will they become world-changers or be involved with abolishing abortion? Will any of the children ever know how God sent Connie and her three young children to pray for their mother while they lay helpless inside their mother's womb? I can only imagine how important their lives must be to Jesus and the wonderful things He has in store for them. It amazes me how Jesus takes such delicate care of every aspect of our lives, during every step of our lives. The Holy Spirit's hand in our lives is so essential and we rarely realize how much He protects us.

There is another thing worth emphasizing. Connie's three young children were by her side and witnessed everything God did in those women. Connie showed her children such a great example of following Jesus to save lives. These are the steps of faith that shape our children's understanding of Christianity. Her children now think it is normal to pray for people in desperate need of Jesus. And it *should* be normal.

We can only imagine how Connie's faith will impact her children's futures to follow Jesus. What sort of great acts of faith and love does God have in store for their futures? One thing is assured— her family's kingdom impact will continue to get better and better. Connie's children, grandchildren, and every generation thereafter will know how to live a blessed life and take a stand against the atrocities of their day.

This entire story of God's hand should make Deuteronomy 7:9 take on a deeper meaning. "Know therefore that the Lord your God is God; he is the faithful God, keeping his covenant of love to a thousand generations of those who love him and keep his commandments."

Connie showed a depth of faith that will continue paying forward forever, in so many ways and in so many lives. On that day, God took Connie's tiny seed of faith and blessed so many people, including her children, the mothers, and the unborn babies. Furthermore, each person impacted will go on to impact others and their families, long after Connie leaves this earth. I call it a kingdom legacy. Connie's name and acts of faith are written in heaven's book, credited to her account with God, never to be erased.

Connie's simple act of faith and love had a domino effect on so many people that day. That's the way God's blessings flow. Only God knows the depth and breadth of her faith's impact. Yet her courageous and simple act of obedience turned out to change so many lives, both now and in the future. Today, Connie still visits abortion clinics in her city and prays for mothers in line. And of course, her children eagerly help.

I must add one thing here. I could have chosen to tell you about all sorts of different examples of great deeds, especially within this chapter where I included some of the most horrific acts of genocide our world has ever seen. There are countless books written and endless stories told about great men and women of God who did wonderful and amazing things in God's kingdom. However, I chose to tell this story about Connie, who is a godly wife and mother of three young children.

On the outside, Connie would appear to be an ordinary housewife who supports her husband, homeschools her children, and loves Jesus. That is exactly why her story is so powerful and impactful. Connie has lots of reasons to believe she could never make a difference in this crazy world. In fact, she could buy into the overwhelmingly popular belief that it's a waste of time to be a stay-at-home mother. She could easily use her education to get a corporate job and let the public school system educate her children and instill its own version of moral values. Thereby giving into the pressures of our culture, which perpetuates a cycle of valuing wealth and short-sighted achievements over our personal responsibility to educate our children and instill biblical values. Allowing the school systems to determine what type of moral compass to instill into her children by brainwashing them with ungodly lies. I can only imagine how drastically different the future would be for Connie's children because of the values Connie has chosen to instill by personally raising her children. She is instilling values that will build a strong nation and a better future.

God loves to work this way. He takes the most unlikely people to do the most amazing things. It shows the world that following His ways result in blessed families and blessed futures. His goodness shines brightest through the most ordinary and faithful people because He alone is God. If we all do our part, God will plant each one of our tiny seeds of faith to change the course of our entire nation. God will take each one of our seemingly small acts of courage and faith to start a chain reaction of hope and life.

This story moved me so deeply that I have told it all over the country to people everywhere. Connie showed such bravery and sincere love for the women in line at that clinic. She didn't try to picket and condemn with bullhorns. Connie showed concern and compassion for the women and their unborn children. From the perspective of those women, Connie was sent by God's very own hand. Furthermore, when Connie placed her caring hands on those women for prayer, God's presence touched those women. I do know one thing: When the presence of God's Spirit touches you, your life will never be the same. There is freedom in the Holy Spirit's presence, and if you follow Jesus, you possess the same life-changing power of God's presence inside of you.

I look forward to the doors God will open for Connie, perhaps giving her a national platform to help remove abortion from our nation's laws, thereby irradicating the spilling of blood onto our nation's soil.

Building God's kingdom happens one soul at a time, but it takes a dedicated effort from all of us. Kingdom building is an impossible task if the entire church depends on just a few to get it done. That's why it is imperative for the entire church to do their part. Then the God-sized task will become a reality and get done.

You can find the first step of your destiny's path by seeking God. Start asking the Holy Spirit: *Give me a heart for the things that grieve You. Open doors of opportunity for me to represent You amongst those who are hurting and crying out to You, oh Lord. Give me the courage to stand up against my own fears so I can leave a kingdom legacy that glorifies Jesus and pays forward forever.*

8

Healing Our Women

We are going to examine an important issue I feel strongly about within our society, and I would be negligent if I left it out. The issue has to do with the oppression of women and the dismissal of their significance within our society and God's kingdom. This chapter is meant to create awareness with the purpose of understanding how we can heal our women, serve our women, and change our distorted cultural mindsets. If you are a woman, this chapter will set you on a path to finding your greatest purposes. If you are a man, you will begin to see women from a different perspective, while learning how to partner with God to help our women find themselves and their most significant place within God's kingdom.

When you look closely at all the wrongdoings in our world, it is obvious to me that Satan is intentionally targeting women. It appears to me he is trying to destroy our women's future, crush their souls, and eliminate their importance from the fabric of our culture.

Being a woman in today's culture seems like a constant uphill battle with opposition from every angle. Fulfilling their fullest God-given potential comes with criticism and closed doors at every turn. Some of the obstacles and challenges include inequality in the workplace and constant opposition from the church about being a minister and a leader. Not to mention bigotry, discrimination, and sexual harassment, just to name a few of the lighter issues.

Women are one of our most precious resources. They are the backbone of our society at every level. They are a foundation for our families and the church. Yet they are underappreciated, and the full potential of their capabilities are too often overlooked.

In a nation plagued with fatherless children, women are raising families alone. When families fall apart, the wives often put the shattered family on their backs to raise fatherless children. When local churches fall apart, it's often the women who step up and put the church on their backs to carry it through hard times. These are contributions that are never fully appreciated. All the while, we ignore the depths of their internal struggles caused by an oppressive and dismissive culture.

On top of all that, women are scrutinized from the very beginnings of childhood. Society has created a twisted version of perfection that's unattainable by any human being. Every feature on a woman is overly criticized, from her body shape, perceived attractiveness, intelligence, and many attributes she's merely born with that cannot be changed.

The daily pressures placed upon women often make them feel inferior deep inside. Their bodies are too skinny or too fat; too short or too tall; too dark or too light. Their hair is too curly or too straight; too red or too brown. Their noses, legs, feet, hands, nails, and everything else needs to be perfect. The amount of pressure for women to achieve a false sense of perfection seems overwhelming from a standard that's void of godly substance and reflects our culture's vile and shallow nature. Perhaps the most damaging effect is the inferiority complex it creates inside our women, a seemingly impossible obstacle to completely overcome.

Women also face issues of inequality in the workplace. Women are expected to do twice the work while receiving minimal recognition. They often need to be twice as smart to get the same jobs, often getting nudged out of top leadership roles from men with half the capabilities and all too often receiving less pay than their male counterparts.

I'm sure there are other wrongs against women that could be listed here. I'm not trying to create an exhaustive list, nor am I trying to explore the depths of each issue. I am merely trying to create awareness and help us realize the totality of the damage. Our society has created a form of oppression against our women through actions that cause deep wounds, while we expect them to push the pain down deep inside, creating layers and layers of unresolved issues. We have hurt our women, and some of those wounds will take a lifetime to heal. Sadly, most of us have contributed in one way or another, most often with the women we are supposed to love the most.

On top of their internal wounds, we even see some women treat each other in the same ways. Instead of supporting and celebrating one another, they often criticize and demean one another. Too often it flows from the insecurities created from our own society. In other words, women often turn on each other for all sorts of insecure reasons, and our society accepts it because everyone else does it.

Unfortunately, the level of oppression goes further than that. Most of our society has created a culture that tries to silence women's voices on many levels. It has only been a little over a hundred years since our nation allowed women to vote. The nineteenth amendment to the U.S. Constitution was ratified on August 18, 1920. It was the last amendment implemented that attempted to remove the extreme levels of discrimination in our culture that were based on color or God-given gender. The Amendment recognized women's God-given rights of equality within our society.

The passage of the nineteenth amendment represented an era when a few brave people were willing to endure persecution and challenge our culture's popular opinion, fighting for our nation to become more aligned with a biblical worldview, at least in the ways we treat each other. By no means am I saying the brutal battles of

137

discrimination ended there. Integrating those freedoms into the fabric of our society has been an entirely different battle, and many great leaders have lost their lives. However, it was our government's last Amendment to allow anything into our Constitution that resembles biblical principles. Allowing women to vote should not have taken our country so long to implement. It sends a loud message that women's proper place in our society is simply unimportant.

We are going to dig a little deeper into some additional issues that are often avoided or kept silenced. To do this, we briefly review a few statistics to better understand some of the tragedies many women face.

Many commonly accepted statistics say that one in five women have been raped at some time in their lives. My experience says these statistics are way too low, by at least two to three times. Most women never report their violators, keeping it pushed down deep inside for their entire life. Many other women live with the pain for thirty or forty years before they let it out. The offense is treated as a taboo subject, bringing shame to the victim instead of the violator. Oftentimes the woman gets the blame or is flat-out called a liar.

Sadly, things get worse for many women. Some endure further violence in their relationships. The National Coalition Against Domestic Violence (NCADV.org) says one in three women have experienced some form of abuse or domestic violence. The most heartbreaking statistic about this abuse is that it occurs most commonly against women between the ages of eighteen and twenty-four. Again, my experience says these statistics are way too low. Many women are not reporting domestic violence because of the same reasons I described above. When friends, family or neighbors become aware of domestic violence, they often ignore it, don't want to get involved, or simply don't care. All the while, more layers of hurt and pain are stacked on women, just to be pushed down deep inside.

One thing about the statistics from rape and domestic abuse that is absolutely true: Little girls are being raped before they reach eighteen years old, only to endure some form of abuse or domestic violence once they reach adulthood. Things seem to go from bad to worse.

I need to create awareness to a big gap in the statistics. The sources of the data gathered concerning rape and domestic violence do not include all Americans who live in our country. Although Native Americans live in America, they are governed by their own tribal laws. Unfortunately, official statistics concerning rape and domestic violence are not available. In my attempt to research rape statistics, I found numbers ranging from 35% to 80% of women on reservations have experienced some form of rape during their lifetime. Again, I could not find an official source, but I can say this. I have personally done missions work on several reservations, and I have several dear friends and kingdom co-laborers who are Natives from reservations in numerous states across the country. All of them tell me the same thing. About 3 out of every 4 women experience rape at some point in their life, with most of it happening with a close family member while girls are under the age of 18. When COVID-19 hit our country, Native men were at home all the time resulting in a significant spike in rape and domestic violence.

I will tell you from personal experience that women and little girls are powerless against their perpetrators. It's often family members who live in the same home. They rarely go to jail, and if they do, it is only for a short time. Then they go right back home, and things get worse from there. It is a seemingly hopeless cycle that usually continues until the girls leave the house. Since the average income in most Native reservations are far below the poverty line, family members are financially helpless. Little girls have nowhere to turn. They are forced to endure rape and domestic violence, leaving them with broken souls and a dwindling prayer of hope for freedom.

While we may not be able to affect tribal laws, God can still use us to bring the healing power of Jesus. The same way He did with Connie and her children from the last chapter. Bringing God's hand into the situation takes prayer, compassion, and courage to help. God will open the doors if we are willing to take a step of faith.

Undoubtedly, the worst part of the statistics in America is the way a woman's voice is silenced. Many times, nobody believes the women who are brave enough to step forward, as if their lives don't matter. When will we allow their voices to be heard without shaming the victims?

There is another unseen problem damaging our women. It has to do with abortion. I know we have covered abortion several times from several different angles. As I stated earlier, it impacts many people in countless ways, and its impact on women is overlooked.

Most of us understand that abortion is the single most horrific act of global genocide in the history of mankind. The effects of it have touched every family in one way or another. But many people seem to ignore the fact that it kills a piece of our women.

Take a moment to view a website that tracks abortion numbers for America and the entire world at www.NumberOfAbortions.com. By the way, it is my understanding that the statistics include Native Americans, since the information does not involve criminal data. After you look at those numbers on the website above, let those numbers sink in for a moment. Each number represents a human being. As bad as that sounds, it doesn't end there. Those numbers also represent all the women who now live with regret, shame, and pain. I'm sure a day will never pass without those mothers thinking about their babies and their decisions. I personally know women who chose to abort their babies. Some of those women are still very young, while other women have aged several decades since they aborted their babies. One thing is common among all the women— their pain never goes away.

Women buy into the lie that says, *It's your body and your decision*. They are told, "*It* is just a lifeless, fleshy blob." Sadly, too many people believe the lies and deception. For some crazy delusional reason, this lie causes our society to downplay the lifetime of pain and shame it creates within mothers who abort their babies. It seems to me that much of our society turns a blind eye to the impact abortion has on women, as if we are subconsciously in denial about its existence or its impact. Oftentimes, mothers who are hurting are offered judgmental criticism instead of healing and prayer.

The tremendous shame forces mothers to push their pain down deep, rarely ever discussing it, forcing them to live with the haunting memories that scar their souls forever.

I wish I could stop here, but the hurt doesn't stop there. Women deal with much more than rape, domestic violence, and abortion. The layers of their lives' heartaches and regrets are stacked higher. However, before I go on, I must say something one more time. This chapter is not meant to paint a grim picture of hopelessness or create an excuse for depression. My goal is to create awareness about the problems many women endure, with the purpose of healing our women and changing the mindset of our distorted culture. I only wish I could say it all differently, perhaps in a better light. It's just such an ugly truth and I only know how to say it one way—the way it is. Saying it any other way would downplay the significance. My stance is this: If I don't say it the way it is, then I'm further contributing to it. Personally, I refuse to contribute in any other way except to champion a change.

Having said that, let's move on to a few more issues requiring awareness and healing.

Have you ever researched divorce rates and the many ways divorce affects families? Divorces create broken homes, broken children, and broken wives and husbands too. Fatherlessness is also caused by premarital sexual relationships, which is another tragedy leaving single mothers to raise children on their own. Fatherless homes damage little girls and boys, making them feel abandoned, often searching for love in all the wrong places for all the wrong reasons. It is a brokenness that often leads to drug addictions, prostitution, debilitating depression, or suicide. Unfortunately, many women fall into these terrible pits and are rendered incapable of fighting their way out. If they do get out alive, there's usually a lifetime of brokenness to recover from, perpetuating a generational cycle with a predisposition for a painful future.

Some women have endured every single tragedy we discussed in this chapter and so much more. Just one of these tragedies is enough to crush a soul. It is hard to imagine how any person can live through several such atrocities and still find the strength to smile. These women look tough on the outside with a seemingly unbreakable exterior. All the while, they are shattered on the inside.

What a shame that many women are not afforded the freedom to allow their fragility to show through. There is a fear inside, telling them the trauma may overtake them. Or even worse, a guarded voice tells them it could happen again.

I hope you are beginning to see the totality of hardships many women endure. The statistics are piled high, and the layers of issues go deep. However, our women are more than a statistic. The women representing each statistic are more than just numbers. Each number represents a woman with a name. Jesus sees her as a soul for whom He sacrificed His life. You may even know of someone who survived some of the things discussed here. We interact with women every day who are harboring pain from these soul-crushing realities. These women could be one of our coworkers, church members, sisters, wives, mothers, or our own daughters.

Our women need us, and they need each other. Not to compare and compete with one another, but to support and build each other up. They need our love, our patience, and our delicate care. Our commitment is needed to walk them through their life's journey of healing, toward new levels of freedom. If God has placed such a woman in your life, take responsibility for her healing. Ask the Lord how you can help her find herself, deep within the layers of deception and lies. That's where a man's real leadership starts.

To all the women reading these words right now, know that you are the heart of our families. Where do you draw such inner strength to live on, after enduring so many layers of suffering and pain? How do you pick up the pieces and still become the heart of our families? I admire you, and I can only imagine what our world could become if we would leverage your strength to help fix our broken nation.

I believe we have entered a new era, where God is healing our women so they can find themselves and find their proper places in every facet of His kingdom. I want to make a prophetic declaration over every woman of God reading this book.

Women of God, it is your time to stand up. God's hand is going to take your extreme brokenness and turn it for good. He has removed you from the hellfire of your past to forge in you a fighter for His kingdom. Jesus turned the tables on Satan's wicked plans of destruction. God is turning your pain into purpose.

Next time that dirty devil whispers a lie into your heart, proclaim this verse from Genesis 50:20 "You intended to harm me, but God

147

intended it for good to accomplish what is now being done, the saving of many lives." You possess a God-appointed destiny that nobody can take away.

I am going to shift gears and talk about women's role in the church because too many women have surrendered their life's destiny to the ill-conceived teachings that limit their God-ordained destiny. I will say this to you concerning the beliefs about women's role in the church—do not believe everything you hear. I'm aware of the restrictions many leaders and denominations put on women. Don't allow it to get inside your soul. God's kingdom cannot afford to lose its most precious resource.

I need to make a statement. Then I want you to research the Bible for yourself. The Bible does not explicitly say that women are not allowed to be leaders of God's church. Jesus didn't say it, nor did Paul make such an explicit statement. Every person who makes such a claim about limiting women's role in the church primarily uses a single passage to build assumptions from. There's a verse in 1 Timothy 2:12 that says, "I do not permit a woman to teach or to assume authority over a man." This verse is directed at husbands and wives. It's aimed at married couples. It's meant for men to assume proper responsibility for leading their wives, while instructing wives to submit to their husbands. That verse has nothing to do with how women function within the church's leadership.

Unfortunately, men have built entire theologies around this single verse, attaching various scriptures to it, attempting to paint a picture of limited authority. As I stated before, there is not one single verse that explicitly states women cannot lead God's church. There are many assumptions made from that single verse in Timothy. Do not make such assumptions when interpreting God's Word, especially an assumption that creates a limitation upon God's church, which is Jesus' most precious possession in the entire universe. In my opinion, it is weak hermeneutics that attempts to patch together an argument using various scriptures and man's deductive reasoning. This weak theology comes from bigotry and self-deluded egos. Seems harsh, I know, but men have created such a law because their egos want to be in charge of everything.

I am fully aware that many people will strongly disagree with my statements. It's just the way I see Scripture, or the lack thereof upon which this limitation on women's role in church is based. There is one thing that is undeniable: The Bible contains many examples of women playing a significant role in God's church throughout much of the New Testament. Women's significance in the church is undeniable.

Frankly, I am amazed that so many people make such bold statements about limiting an entire gender from their rightful roles in God's kingdom. Sadly, we will never know the full damage caused to godly women over the countless years of our shortsighted beliefs that have somehow turned into biblical law. Even more tragic, we will never know the depths to which we have crippled God's church from its full potential.

Whether you are a man or woman reading this, I urge you to go back to the Bible with a clear mind and a clean slate of thinking. Instead of going into Scripture looking to validate your beliefs, allow the Word to speak for itself. Jesus doesn't mince His words, nor does the Bible do so about such crucial things. If Jesus forbids women from leading His church, His Word would explicitly state it because the church is that important to Him.

Now I don't claim to have all the answers about how God is maturing His church to a fuller expression. But there is one thing I do know: We are getting it wrong when it comes to women leaders in the church. I challenge you to explore the answer for yourself instead of allowing popular opinion to sway you. I have personally asked the Lord to allow me to be part of His plans to help women find their rightful place, and it is by far my proudest contribution to God's kingdom to-date.

I said all of that to say this: Woman of God, do not allow such beliefs to cloud your mind or limit your divine destiny. By no means am I telling you to create discord and division within the church body. The church belongs to Jesus, and nobody has the right to damage her. We are not going to change the mindset of our local church or even our pastor. That is God's job. Instead, dare to find your true identify and muster the courage to be yourself. The you can rest assured that your best destiny will find you.

I want to pause here for a moment. If you have personally dealt with some or all of the horrible things above, it's important for you to get help working through them. Many of the issues we discussed in this chapter are life altering. You likely need a qualified Christian counselor who uses biblically based methods that are Christ centered. You cannot fully heal until you intentionally work through your heartache.

Here is why I want to emphasize Christian counseling. I personally know hundreds of women who have endured many of the things I've listed in this chapter. A small number of those women received consistent counseling, and unfortunately, most of them have not. Their lives are a cycle of blow-ups, meltdowns, and brief counseling from a person they trust the most. Since trust is another major obstacle, they usually find an excuse to discontinue or avoid counseling altogether. The most unfortunate situation occurs when they disqualify every single person who can help, which is typically a sign that there is massive damage that needs focused healing from a trained and highly experienced counselor.

Many women who have experienced unspeakable tragedies avoid counseling altogether. While it is true the Holy Spirit will heal you over time, avoidance can lead to decades of inner turmoil. That's why it so important. It allows God's healing hand in your life.

Healing comes from three places—the Spirit of God, the Word of God, and people of God. God is certainly able to heal without using people, but it can take decades instead of a few short years with counseling. Jesus chooses to work through His divine family. Therefore, the roadblock often lies within our willingness or unwillingness to face our past. Trust is usually the first steps on the road to healing.

If you are currently suffering from the pain of your past, there is no doubt that God will still use you. However, we limit our own level of usefulness to God when we refuse healing. There are places within you that overreact, over scrutinize, or just plain view from an incorrect perspective. Many things become about our feelings, how we were offended, or even worse, that we are unworthy. Simply put, we become highly susceptible to demons playing with our mind and emotions to manipulate us. Our reactions can cause damage to our most important relationships. Demonic tactics can keep us imprisoned within our own mind to hold us back from divine opportunities. We can become a puppet, while being tossed back and forth with lies and deception.

In short, the consequences of refusing or discrediting the need for counseling can result in a shackled life that often keeps us on an emotional rollercoaster. As I stated before, Christian counseling can be the difference between receiving healing over the course of years versus decades. We will experience a more enjoyable and peaceful life for us and the ones we love the most.

If you have been through adversity, there is probably some aspect of what I stated that applies to you. If you are unable to see it, ask your spouse or someone close to you. Get input from someone who loves you because your perspective may be blurred and distorted. We are often unable to see ourselves with the clarity that Jesus sees us.

If you have someone in your life who needs healing, start asking the Holy Spirit to show you how to be part of her healing. If your wife needs healing, the husband is responsible to care for her, help her, and guide her toward healing. Husbands often feel helpless in this and maybe even highly frustrated. Many times, the only thing we can do is ask God to change us so we can begin treating the women in our lives with the patience and care of Jesus. There's nothing that will heal our wives except the hand of God. The most life-changing action we can take is allowing Jesus to change us. Then our wives will open their heart for Jesus' healing touch.

As a husband, I assume full responsibility for my wife's healing. I never stop praying. I never stop seeking for God to change me, to change the way I see my wife and change the way I treat my wife. I also teach my sons, spiritual sons, and countless men I mentor to do the same. I only say these things because I want all men to do the same. I believe it is every husband's responsibility to lead our wives, by serving their needs.

None of this is easy. On the contrary, it is usually the most difficult thing we will ever do, both for the husband helping his wife and for the wife needing healing. Our internal fight is often the toughest journey of our walk with Jesus; yet it is also the most rewarding victory, especially for the ones we love the most.

There is so much more I could say about healing, or the internal pain that tragedies cause, or even the problems it can cause in marriages, families, and ministry. However, this chapter is not meant to provide complete healing or explore the depths and effects of each tragedy. The purpose is twofold: Get women on a road toward healing and drive men into action to help heal our women. Perhaps we could even dare to allow the Lord to change our mindset about women and their place in our culture and God's kingdom.

Nonetheless, healing should start today. Some of you women had your innocence stolen, your purity ravaged, or your hearts crushed by those who were supposed to love you the most. The evil inside men has created brokenness, suffering, and pain that can seem beyond repair. It leaves little girls lost before they are adults, and it creates women who feel broken beyond repair. They endure the worst nightmares and still manage to find inner strength to trudge through the aftermath. They possess amazing strength to fight forward.

Our society needs our women to be whole and healthy on every level. These deep wounds often take a lifetime of healing. Some of the deepest wounds may never completely heal. Either way, there is hope for a new life, a different life of peace on the inside and tranquility on the outside. Find healing that allows you to experience a bright future.

Healing and forgiveness are rarely achieved overnight. The path is a journey of steps and pieces. Although healing and forgiveness are both intertwined, they are separate. Unforgiveness shackles our soul and keeps us in bondage, attached to pain. It keeps our healing bound within its grips. Forgiveness releases our healing. It is the part we play to find freedom from within. It is a key that we can control, and we alone possess it.

There is an answer for our heartache. There is hope for us to live an unhindered life filled with peace. Again, there's no better time than now to begin our journey toward healing. From now on, when someone hurts you, refuse the urge to fight with harsh words or hurtful reactions. Revenge is not the answer. Pain for pain never works. We must fight with forgiveness and pray for people who hurt us. Start praying for people who have hurt you in the past. Every time that person who hurt you the most comes to mind, say a prayer for them.

Praying for our enemies puts those demons on notice. It sends a loud message that says, *Whenever you try to whisper negativity into my heart, I will respond with righteousness.* Our actions of

157

forgiveness make room for God to work inside our hearts and within every person who hurts us.

Do your part to stop the vicious cycle of hurt and pain. Each step we take toward forgiveness is another step we take toward deeper levels of freedom. Each step we take toward inner healing takes us closer to our biggest God-destiny. Each one of those past situations has made us stronger. God uses our past circumstances and bad decisions to mold us. Our journey toward forgiveness will make us more effective in God's kingdom. This inner fight will make us more useful to God. Draw on the strength you've gained from overcoming the darkness of your past. Allow it to deepen your faith so you can see a face of Jesus you never knew.

We may never understand the reasons for tragedies that happened in our life. At times, we may not believe that good things can come out of our life's toughest moments. One thing is for sure, tragedies can break us if we respond incorrectly. So let your faith shine during the hardest of times. There are many things throughout our life that are beyond our control, but we can control the way we respond to difficult situations. When we respond correctly, we will see a face of God's grace we never knew before and it will forever change us.

God does not promise that everything will go smoothly. But He does promise to be there for us during life's toughest storms—to protect us, keep us, and carry us through.

The only hope for freedom from our past pains is Jesus. He can use our past to propel us into our purpose. God makes a way when there is no way. Jesus creates purpose from our pain. He's so masterful at it.

Ask yourself, what are the steps you need to take toward forgiveness: Do I need to forgive right now, at this very moment? Is it my father, a relative, a spouse, or my perpetrator? Have you verbalized your forgiveness to yourself and the one who hurt you? It might be the most difficult and painful thing you have ever done, but it will be the most liberating moment for your new life. Now is your moment to confront and conquer in a healthy way, so you can move forward into a new light.

How do we start? By facing our demons head-on with Jesus' own words, spoken to us with healing in mind. "But to you who are

159

listening I say: Love your enemies, do good to those who hate you, bless those who curse you, pray for those who mistreat you" (Luke 6:26-28).

Besides, revenge is not our place. It is the Lord's responsibility. Romans 12:19 says, "Do not take revenge, my dear friends, but leave room for God's wrath, for it is written: 'It is mine to avenge; I will repay,' says the Lord."

This verse has serious consequences from the hand of our Creator against those who mistreat others or hurt God's people. It's a big reason we need to pray for God's forgiveness. God's eternal punishment for those who mistreat you will never heal your soul. Only grace and love can do that. Love is the key, not revenge and hate.

If you love Jesus, then you have been given a second chance for restoration. If you have accepted Jesus into your heart and you strive for an ever-growing relationship with Him, you have become renewed. Your purity and innocence have been restored. But this time around, it's a holy purity. It's a godly innocence. Your purity and innocence have been given back by God's own loving hand because Jesus put His blood over it, so you can be free.

Jesus has done much more than merely restore things Satan stole from you. He has given back much more than you had before. Jesus has made you holy from the inside out. You now possess a heavenly treasure, and He has many more treasures in store for you.

This is your time to face your past with courage. Starting today, begin marching toward your new future with courage and confidence. The wind of God is at your back. With God, you can do all things.

How will you take a stand against your deepest pains, biggest fears, and strongest insecurities?

The Holy Spirit is doing many things within His church and throughout the entire earth. He is taking us to new levels of faith, power, and unity. In this new era, the Lord is placing women in their proper places in every part of our culture. I believe God will begin elevating women into places of significant influence and leadership. First, we will see God begin to heal our women, so they can find themselves and find their proper places in our homes, churches,

161

businesses, and every area in our culture. I believe it's the heart of God to do this.

Our entire society would be a stronger and better place with women as an integral part of it. We should be asking ourselves, *What can I do to help the women in my life to find their best self and their biggest destiny? How can I be their voice? What are God's plans for their lives and how can I support their healing and God's destiny for them? How can I help them find confidence and courage? What areas of my life does God need to change so I can be a better help? Where can I become involved with support organizations or ministries that help women in my city or nation?*

Take a moment of focused time to reflect on the things in this chapter. Do your own research using the Bible, books, internet, etc., and become more educated on these issues. Most importantly, spend time alone with the Holy Spirit. Seek His voice and His heart on these things. Ask the Lord to help you figure out how to be part of His plans to change these things in your own life or the lives of those around you.

Celebrate the women in your life and thank God for them. Make it a priority to help our women achieve everything God has for them.

9

Fame and Fortune

There seems to be a hidden force driving Americans toward power and greed, an internal drive that wakes us up in the morning and makes us feel as if we are already behind schedule before we get out of bed. It keeps our minds racing at night to keep looking into the future, fixated on tomorrow's success. It's some type of inner drive that speaks into our souls and says, "Keep going higher" or "You should be doing better." It keeps pushing us to make us feel as though enough is never enough.

This inner drive is often a sign from underlying issues that draw us toward our own definition of success for the wrong reasons. We all have given in to the wrong motives at different levels during various times in our lives. Wealth, power, and fame drive people to make selfish decisions that are unethical, illegal, or just downright destructive. Such decisions are outright sinful. You may be reading this and won't even consider that your *little white lies* are sinful, or you may believe they will never hurt anyone. But a sin is a sin, and all sin hurts someone. The effects of our sins either hurt ourselves, our families, or God. Perhaps we are unable to see it, or we refuse to see it. Either way, it could mean that we have something hidden inside our heart that needs to be removed. I call it a blind spot, and the only One who can take it out is the hand of God.

I heard an old adage while I was in Europe on business for several months. It goes something like this: *Americans live to work, and Europeans work to live.* When you compare the emphasis Americans put on our dreams and careers, you will see how imbalanced and distracted we are from the most important things in life. Our society's values are overly focused on personal achievements and hinge on our own definition of success. Those types of self-centered values conflict with God's character. Are our dreams more important than our family?

A fine line exists when pursuing success that can become an obsession. Unfortunately, those lines have become blurred and distorted in our culture today. Our nation has tipped the scales of

God's priorities for our life toward a gluttonous appetite for. No doubt, God created this planet on which we can live a blessed life in the presence of our almighty God. But the spiritual forces driving us toward our hollow obsessions are undeniable. Satan has distorted God's definition of blessings. We now equate blessings with wealth, comfort, and a twisted version of *happiness*. I believe we became most aware of it during the COVID pandemic, as if God was trying to recalibrate our priorities.

For example, the U.S. loves to flaunt her wealth and put it on display for the world to see. It is a brash display of possessing more than everyone else. Our egocentric actions say, "Look at me. I am the best, the wealthiest, the strongest, and the most successful." Our Facebook and Instagram pages say it, and our materialistic lives try to prove it with our big cars, big houses, and big paychecks.

Materialistic possessions are not bad within themselves. However, we are at the extreme end of the spectrum. We take it to another level of expectation, as if we are entitled to special treatment. It seems like many Americans feel as if somebody owes us something just because we are Americans.

Our nation has become shallow, and its foundation has become a façade—a foundation that's empty and devoid of God's true eternal blessings. How did we become such shallow human beings?

I pray we learn a different definition of success than we have been programmed to believe. Success is not defined in the eyes of the beholder. Success is not subject to our own definition. We cannot create our own brand of success. God created the rules, and we are privileged to live by them. This is His world. He created it and He created us. God rules over all things, no matter how entitled we think we are. There is one thing we are entitled to, though. We are entitled to live by God's ways. We are privileged to walk a life of integrity, equality, and generosity. God's ways are an honor to follow, not burdensome requirements. His ways are the only path that ensures we will live our best and blessed lives.

Jesus' blood made the way for our freedom, and when we live according to God's ways it ensures we will remain free on the inside. The privileges we are afforded cost Jesus His life. Our freedom was not free.

We will now discuss how the wrong motives affect our pursuit of wealth and success. Our nation's chronic problem with dysfunctional families has created deep rooted issues in a generation that thinks they need success to feel good about themselves. These issues cause people to pursue success and wealth for the wrong reason. If we have the wrong motives, we will sacrifice our integrity to get what we want. Our integrity defines our character, and our character reveals our heart's motives. Corrupt motives create corrupt people.

There should be more to our dreams than wealth and fame. Wealth, success, and fame are not necessarily bad things, nor is it a sin to have lots of money. The sin comes from the things we are willing to do for money or success.

The Bible says in 1 Timothy 6:10, "For the love of money is a root of all kinds of evil. Some people, eager for money, have wandered from the faith and pierced themselves with many griefs."

Some of us may think we don't have issues with greed or a love of money. However, everyone has issues that lie hidden inside. I call them blind spots. Fame and fortune have a way of revealing our blind spots.

Perhaps our issues never came to light because we never had much money or fame. Nonetheless, deep issues could exist inside our hearts. Most likely, there are small telltale signs that have gone unnoticed. Whether we are aware of our own issues, wealth and fame always reveal character flaws. Our heart issues are the source of internal struggles that plague our soul. Oftentimes, they cause the most harm when we possess wealth or fame. Deep-hearted issues can stem from a dysfunctional past or painful situations that create deep roots and scars on our soul. If left unchecked, some roots can become a cancer, eating our soul and devouring our life.

What things lie dormant inside of you that God needs to remove? Take a few moments to pray and ask the Holy Spirit to reveal things He wants to take out of you. Ask Him to reveal your motives, priorities, and character.

I've listed a few situations that will help reveal issues inside of you. Before you read the following questions, take a few moments to pray and ask the Holy Spirit to reveal things He wants to take out of you. Ask Him to reveal a deeper meaning of these questions and

169

show you where you need to refocus your intentions, priorities, and character.

- Does your job constantly take you away from spending time with God or your family? Do you justify it as putting your family's needs first?
- Are you willing to manipulate your way to the top?
- Have you cheated someone out of their money or dealt unethically in a business deal?
- Have you intentionally used someone else to move toward your dream or to gain notoriety?
- Do your plans of success put you at the center of attention?
- Do your successes or achievements make you feel better about yourself?

Make time to reflect on these questions, with an eye toward uncovering hidden blind spots within yourself.

Here's an example of hidden blind spots that revealed themselves during hard times many of us faced. During the COVID-19 pandemic, the entire planet was turned upside down. Lots of people lost their jobs and their health. Others lost their businesses, while so many others lost close family members. It was a turbulent time of uncertainty and instability. All these things caused fear and anxiety, which became a driving force that created chaos, looting, and violence. It touched everyone on numerous fronts that ultimately tested our faith and our character. Unfortunately, many people failed that test when COVID-19 hit hard.

Those who were hit the hardest found themselves lying, cheating, and stealing to sustain their families. Some people literally looted stores, while others found ways to extort money from the government's stimulus programs. Moments like these will either uncover a corrupt heart or they will strengthen your faith and refine your character.

What did you learn about your faith and character during the COVID pandemic? Did you cheat, lie, or steal to obtain things that benefitted you or your family?

If any of these issues of character apply to you, there's no doubt you need to address them, immediately. You probably have deeper issues buried within the depths of your heart. If the roots remain unchecked, their grip can get out of control and overtake you.

Regardless of whether things get out of control, unchecked issues will hold us back from being more useful to God, and our growth can stagnate.

Our goal should be constant growth and maturity so we can become more useful to the hand of God. Let's look at Jesus' words in Luke 16:10-11 to better understand the importance of the things we've discussed. "Whoever can be trusted with very little can also be trusted with much, and whoever is dishonest with very little will also be dishonest with much. So, if you have not been trustworthy in handling worldly wealth, who will trust you with true riches?"

According to Jesus' expectations, we will never reach our most significant God-given destiny if we possess low integrity and poor character. If God is unable to trust us with small things, then our level of usefulness will never grow in God's eyes. We basically become incapable of handling significant responsibility for God or His kingdom. Our lives either become stagnate, we fall backwards, or something worse happens. We manipulate our way to higher levels of responsibility beyond our level of capability. How do we know if we have been promoted beyond our level of capability?

Usually, we create chaos and become the source of contention, while broken relationships lie in our path to the top.

The worst outcome could be that we fall backwards and pull away from God. Or we could experience a life full of frustrations, dead ends, or meaningless successes.

God has His own version of wealth and success. It involves managing God's kingdom and representing Jesus. In fact, Jesus spoke about wealth and success in a parable in Luke 19:13-17. "'Put this money to work,' he said, 'until I come back.' . . . The first one said, 'Sir, your mina has earned ten more.' 'Well done, my good servant!' his master replied. 'Because you have been trustworthy in a very small matter, take charge of ten cities.'"

Jesus wraps up the parable with this statement in Luke 19:26; "I tell you that to everyone who has, more will be given, but as for the one who has nothing, even what they have will be taken away. But those enemies of mine who did not want me to be king over them – bring them here and kill them in front of me."

These verses clearly show that Jesus gives us the responsibility to manage wealth and authority in a way that impacts His kingdom.

The verses also make it clear that Jesus has an expectation for us to run His kingdom according to His ways. Otherwise, our level of usefulness in His kingdom will be limited, at best. The worst thing that could happen, is that our corruption takes over and it eventually costs us our life.

The level of our kingdom impact is the key to true success. There is more to our kingdom assignment than wealth and success. Wealth and success are not the goal, nor are they a measuring stick for success. They should only be views as tools to advance biblical Christianity in our culture. As I stated in a previous chapter, true wealth is something money cannot buy, and death can't take away.

The world has created a false measuring stick for success that creates a temporal mindset measured by our personal earnings or self-centered achievements. Our culture's version of success is the opposite of Jesus' expectations. Every form of success that's devoid of God's purposes is shallow and completely self-centered. God's measuring stick for success creates an eternal mindset that puts others first and places our trust in Jesus. God's ways allow blessings to flow into our lives and those blessings overflow onto everyone around us. We become a blessing of generosity and love. This free flow of blessings brings peace deep within our souls.

Look at Mark 9:35. The twelve disciples were arguing about who was the greatest. Their egos got in the way and blinded their kingdom perspective. While they were debating, Jesus told them, "Anyone who wants to be the first must be the very last, and the servant of all."

These scriptures mean we are most effective when we have the biggest impact within other people's lives. Our kingdom assignment always involves helping others get to the place God wants them. This is the example that Jesus established while He lived and the very reason He died.

On the contrary, the world says you must achieve your personal dreams at any cost. As you can see, a kingdom mindset is directly opposed to the self-centered mindset of our society.

As we get better at allowing Jesus to change our mindsets, God's ways gradually overtake our inner selves. Then Jesus will give us increasing levels of responsibility.

175

What does this all mean? It means our goals should be focused on moving ourselves aside to become more impactful within God's kingdom. Pursuing God' plans and purposes before our own, for the sake of serving the needs of others, will make us the most effective in our lifetimes of serving Jesus. John the Baptist said it best in John 3:30: "He [Jesus] must become greater; I must become less."

If you allow God's ways to guide your life, eternal success is certain, and wealth may come. But how do Jesus' expectations for success compare with our nation's ideals of success?

Much of the world sees Americans as having an inborn sense of entitlement, and we act as if the universe revolves around us. It fuels our big egos. We blindly equate cockiness with confidence, and we sadly think it's one of our best strengths.

Our nation's egocentric mindset has gone way too far. It exists in every corner of our culture, and it has infected everything we accomplish. Our distorted mindset is woven into the fabric of our entire culture, like a cancer eating every part of our lives from the inside out.

It couldn't be more apparent than in corporate America. Top executives in corporate America manipulate their way to the top of the corporate ladder in a game of politics, where careers are won and lost. Futures can come to an end before they get started if you are unable to navigate through the rough waters. There's a familiar adage that says, Only the strong survive in the business world, and the weak get eaten. My translation of this adage would be, The ethical and naïve are overtaken by the corrupt.

Too many global companies and powerful executives will do anything to gain the edge or take what they want—in a game of kill or be killed. However, high level executives and global companies are not the only places unethical practices happen. They happen at every level of business. Unethical business practices have become commonplace. Manipulating your way into a position by lying or slandering someone else to make yourself look good is much more common than it should be.

Most people do not usually begin their careers with plans of corruption in their future. Nobody devises sinister plans of destroying careers to get to the top when they first enter the job

177

market. It usually starts with a little white lie or a seemingly innocent cover-up of some sort. One thing can lead to another if your character flaws are left unchecked. The path is a long journey of several tiny steps of compromise. All those tiny steps add up over a long period of time. Then we end up in a place we never intended to go, and we're not even sure how we arrived as such a place. We could turn into somebody we never planned to be and doing things we never imagined doing. Demons use the journey of missteps to turn us away from God and His ways. We end up doing it all for money, position, or fame.

If any of us believes we are immune from it, we are fooling ourselves. The journey of corruption is not a straight line. It happens in small steps of compromise, while maneuvering our way toward our big goals. Before we know it, we dislike the face we see in the mirror. Our life reflects a different version of ourselves, a person whose values have been compromised. Compromised values create blurred boundaries. Right and wrong become unclear.

We could lose ourselves and lose sight of true wealth. Truth becomes self-defined, while our values become unscrupulous. Our identity gets lost within a sea of immoral values.

There is a long list of companies where these things happened to executives—leaders who embezzled millions, lied to investors, or manipulated the company's financial earnings to artificially inflate stock prices. Some of the most infamous cases are the Enron scandal in 2001, the Theranos scandal in 2018, and the multiple scandals from Goldman and Sachs. We'll take a brief look at each situation to better understand the condition of our business world.

Enron employed over twenty thousand employees with a reported gross annual income of $1.3 billion in the year 2000. The organization became the seventh largest company in America. In 2001, the company declared bankruptcy after reports surfaced about manipulated financial reports and fraudulent accounting practices. Audits revealed embezzlement by the executive staff that cost shareholders $74 billion. The scandal led to lost jobs and billions stolen from retirement money and benefits. It was the largest scandal ever uncovered in corporate America's history, at that time. In the end, the employees were robbed of their lifetime retirement savings and left out in the cold.

Another company, Theranos, was founded in 2003 by Elizabeth Holmes when she was only nineteen years old. Elizabeth was seen as a genius business prodigy expected to change the world. However, in 2018, Theranos was charged with an elaborate plan of long-term fraud by the U.S. Securities and Exchange Commission. The CEO (Elizabeth) and the President were both charged with deceiving investors about their product. The two leaders made claims to investors about developing a highly technical product with groundbreaking capabilities, when in reality, they never developed the technology into a fully functional product. The leaders created an entire organization that was somehow valued at $10 billion, and it was all based on the leaders' fraudulent claims.

Theranos employed a brilliant team of engineers to create a product capable of conducting multiple laboratory blood tests. Their small and relatively inexpensive product was the size of a personal printer, and it was supposed to replace a room full of laboratory machines worth millions of dollars. To top off their exaggerated claims, the two leaders said their product could cut normal testing time down to hours instead of days, a seemingly impossible scientific achievement.

Unfortunately, even the company's brilliant engineering team was never able to get the product off the R&D testing bench. Nonetheless, Theranos's leaders continued making deliberate claims that their fully functioning product was being mass produced.

The company kept raising the stakes on making increasingly higher claims of functionality. Nonetheless, as years passed by, the leaders made claims of increasing the product capabilities, as if they were creating newer and better versions when in fact, they never delivered a single product to any customer during their fifteen years of false promises. It was all an effort to keep the money flowing from investors. After years of deceiving investors and would-be clients, the CEO and President raised a total of $700 million in cash. It was such a twisted story Netflix made a documentary about it.

I'm sure the CEO never made plans to scam $700 million as a young nineteen-year-old prodigy. It always starts out with small steps of compromise that eventually create a corrupt character. The longer it goes unchecked, the worse it becomes. As time goes on, the corrupt character continues rationalizing higher levels of deception, dishonesty, and fraud.

Perhaps the biggest scam of all came from Goldman and Sachs. They are a juggernaut when it comes to investment banking, securities, and wealth management. This company has the power and influence to manipulate the entire stock market. Unfortunately, they have a long history of corruption, including executives who embezzled money, used offshore tax havens, conducted money laundering, manipulated stock prices, and created a scheme that played a part in the collapse of the housing market in 2007-2008. The company's scheme allowed them to profit from the collapse that caused a U.S. recession. To top it off, they ended up using government bailout money to provide their executives with bonuses, while the rest of America was foreclosing on their homes and losing their 401(k) retirement lifetime savings. It was a wicked plan, allowing their top executives to cash in on the misery of our entire country.

Conduct your own research on the numerous claims against Goldman and Sachs. It seems as if they created a culture of greed and power at any cost. The company still does business today and grossed $5.2 billion in 2019. Somehow, the organization finds ways to endure multiple cases of fraud and embezzlement. To an outsider looking in, it appears they are somehow being protected. I am not a conspiracy theorist type of person, but if I had to guess, based on the history I read about this company, I would dare to say there are payoffs and backdoor deals being made to keep the company intact. When there are piles of cash to go around and the stakes for our economy are high, corruption finds a way of rationalizing itself.

These are examples of extreme situations of corruption in our business world. Unfortunately, these situations are way too common. Each of these companies have one thing in common: greedy people with a ravenous appetite for wealth and power at any cost. Their appetite eventually consumes every shred of personal ethics and moral values. There are no words to describe these men and women who have caused so much despair in the lives of so many. Evil intentions worthy of God's judgment have created a culture that keeps pushing the immoral boundaries of our nation.

I'm sure these companies started out on a good path with good intentions and high ethical standards. They planned on doing things the right way. But somehow, little by little, tiny steps of compromise turned into all-out corruption. The pressure started chipping away at their integrity. A lack of character makes way for destruction. That's how big dreams turn into bad nightmares.

Abraham Lincoln said it best: "If you want to test a man's character, give him power."

Hopefully, you are beginning to see the need for a good moral foundation built upon God's ways. Suffice it to say, we must maintain biblical integrity during our journeys toward fulfilling dreams and visions of success. God's ways keep us safe and protect us from harming ourselves or others. That's why it so important to address our inner self before we go out and try to conquer the world, achieve great success, or gain big wealth. Be at peace with yourself and God. There are too many broken people driven to succeed for all the wrong reasons. This is especially true for folks who have a distorted view of themselves and of God and His grace.

If our self-perception or self-image is distorted, we become an easy target for the enemy. Demons will lay traps of deception to manipulate us. They will fill our head with lies and tell us success will fix all the things broken, both within and around us. We cannot allow ourselves to fall into the enemy's trap of believing such shallow things. Fame and fortune will never be enough to fill our emptiness, our insecurities, or our appetite for success.

There is nothing on this earth that will ever fill the voids within, except the love of Jesus. Achieving big goals or attaining fancy titles will never be enough to fulfill us. Only the blood of Jesus can make us enough. Shallow endeavors will only leave us feeling unsatisfied and wanting more. Our appetite will only grow deeper.

Become comfortable with who you are today, without accolades, fame, wealth, or popularity. Understand and accept your eternal value in the eyes of our Creator. Personal success is a shallow journey, and it will never define us. It will never change the perception of ourselves. Achievements cannot make us a better

185

person. We will never be enough with success, until we are enough without it. Only Jesus can fill the voids of our heart.

Following Jesus is the only journey deep enough to fulfill us, and it will take all our strength and courage to see it through. We will spend our lifetime uncovering the treasures Jesus has in store for us. But it will cost us everything, so hold onto your wealth and possessions with a loose hand. Be willing to let it all go without hesitation, and we will be assured the enemy will lose his grip of influence over us. Keep in mind that courage is key: courage to be wrong, courage to stand up when we see wrongdoings and courage to fail. Always remember that courage is not the absence of fear but the determination to fight through adversity and overcome.

God's plans for our success go much deeper than our tiny imaginations can conjure up. There is more substance to God's plans than our personal goals will ever reach. God's plans are undeniably more satisfying than any shallow achievements that bring money or fame. His plans create eternal wealth, while our plans create temporary happiness that never lasts.

Before you take another step toward God's biggest destiny for your life, it's important that you focus on a more important journey. You must be healthy and whole within before you create personal goals of success. Otherwise, you could be setting yourself up for disappointment, or worse, the biggest fall of your life.

Success will never create our identity, make us fit in, or give us a sense of belonging. If our identity or self-worth is dependent on our achievements and successes, we will never be enough. It's a shallow measuring stick. Our self-worth will always be tied to the waves of our life's ups and downs. Being comfortable inside our own skin is a critical part of being whole and healthy. We do not need success or great achievements to feel important or whole. Be okay with who you are without those things, or you will never feel whole with those things.

Begin to embrace who you are today—your background, your brokenness and weaknesses, and where you have come from. Embracing our personal God-story tells the world about the goodness of Jesus Christ. God's strength shines brightest when we allow ourselves to be comfortable with our weaknesses and a dependence on God.

I believe this is exactly what Paul meant in 2 Corinthians 12:9-11, "But [Jesus] said to me, 'My grace is sufficient for you, for my power is made perfect in weakness.' Therefore, I will boast all the more gladly about my weaknesses, so that Christ's power may rest on me. That is why, for Christ's sake, I delight in the weaknesses, in insults, in hardships, in persecutions, in difficulties. For when I am weak, then I am strong."

The power of God is displayed through our weaknesses. It sounds backwards, but God works opposite of the world's self-centered mindset. The world says we need to be strong and take advantage of the weak. God says we need to depend on Him while we serve those who are less fortunate.

The fact is, we are still the same person inside whether we are rich or poor, educated or illiterate, famous or unknown, influential or insignificant. We should never allow opinions from others to define us, whether negatively or positively. When we are in a state of mind where we embrace every part of our strengths and weaknesses, we become open to a new healthy mindset that will not allow someone else's perception to penetrate our soul.

Our most difficult journey lies within the depths of our heart's darkest and most painful places. Conversely, our life's biggest achievements are accomplished when God transforms our mind and heart. Life's biggest journey is the one within.

There is one last vital thing we need to clarify before ending this chapter. I mentioned it a few times without defining it because I wanted to build up to it. I'm talking about our level of usefulness to God. For some reason, we rarely hear anyone talk about it and I don't know why.

Our level of usefulness determines where and how God can utilize our life. Our level of usefulness is key to our kingdom impact. It's somehow tied to the degree of freedom we have from our internal issues. Internal issues limit our usefulness to God and the impact we can have on His kingdom. We need freedom from our past; from roots of rejection, pride, ego, and shame; from the love of money; from victimized spirits; and from a long list of selfish desires and internal chains that lie within our hearts and are attached to our

189

souls. Demons lose their influence over us as we gain more freedom from these issues.

As we become less susceptible to demonic influence, we become more usefulness to God's plans and purposes. Our degree of freedom is supposed to grow over time, as our commitment to Jesus deepens. It's part of the journey as a Christian . . . just like Abraham's journey. The journey into the depths of our hearts is the most rewarding journey with Jesus.

To take it a step further, we will look at a few godly men and women God has asked to give their lives for the name of Jesus and the advancing the gospel. Their acts of such heroic selflessness have advanced Christianity forever and instilled courage into the hearts of believers everywhere.

Stephen was the first Christian from the early church to give his life. He died with such grace and humility, while being assaulted with stones at the hands of his own countrymen. As Stephen gasped for his last breath, he asked Jesus to forgive his murderers. Stephen gave grace to his murders because Jesus gave *him* grace. What a selfless act of honor. It was the ultimate honor that Jesus would see fit to allow Stephen to die for His name. Stephen was willing to give the ultimate sacrifice . . . himself. His usefulness to God came without boundaries or selfish expectations. Stephen embraced persecution with a kingdom-focused mentality.

Laying down our lives to follow Jesus means so much more than we think. It's the ultimate privilege; the ultimate honor; for the ultimate cause. Where will we stand in times of controversy?

The bigger our sacrifice, the bigger our impact. Most of us are not prepared to risk our life for God's kingdom at this moment. However, the story of our life is not over.

Another person in the Bible who gave his life is Peter. Peter's impact on God's kingdom is immeasurable. What I love most about Peter's story is how he failed, got back up, and turned his life into a success story. His faith didn't start out so strong. He denied ever knowing Jesus after they captured Jesus to kill Him. But later in Peter's life, he died fulfilling Jesus' Great Commission. He gave his life and was crucified for the advancement of Christianity. Peter thought it was such an honor to die for Jesus that he refused to be crucified in the same manner as Jesus. Peter was crucified on a cross upside down because he felt unworthy to die in the same manner as Jesus had died. Peter's journey was not over when he denied knowing Jesus three times. Jesus confronted Peter about his mistake, and Peter humbled himself by allowing Jesus to reconcile their relationship. Peter learned a valuable lesson that launched him into his most impactful destiny. It was the beginning of a deeper journey that culminated with Peter's death. Serving God is an honor and a privilege, not a sacrifice.

Dare to reach beyond yourself to touch God's dreams. Start by asking God what His plans and purposes are and begin seeking His help to make you more useful for those things. The best way to become more useful is by learning to forgive. If we are always offended or have a hard time forgiving people who hurt us, we will never be very useful to God. Start praying for those who offend you and ask God to remove the root of offense from within. Treat those who hurt you with kindness, patience, and practice self-control. If you mess up, ask the Lord to give you more opportunities to grow and get it right.

Ask the Lord for courage to follow God's greatest purposes for your life. Dare to be more useful to Jesus' plans and purposes.

Spend some time alone with God to reflect on the things within this chapter. Ask the Holy Spirit to reveal your blind spots and the areas you struggle with. Allow His Spirit to penetrate the deepest corners of your heart. Make your heart transparent in the presence of God and seek His voice to discover how you can become more useful to God right now. Ask the Lord, Which area of my heart do I need to take a stand? Strive for consistent growth in your love for Jesus and dedication to His cause.

Dare to take a stand for God's ways.

10

A Drifting Culture

In this chapter, we will review some of the most influential elements of our everyday culture that have changed the course of our nation. We will explore areas in our culture that are broken and discover how Satan is trying to use our broken culture to destroy us. We are reviewing several elements of our culture, but we are only taking a high-level overview. Doing a deep dive analysis into every part of our culture is unnecessary. My objective is to reveal how the individual elements of our culture work together to shape our society.

Satan has a diabolical plan that is much bigger than any of us realize—a plan that is very complex and highly organized. His plan involves ruling the earth and destroying mankind by turning us against God. To carry out his diabolical plan, he has organized an army of fallen angels and created a hierarchy with the same mission. Every move he makes has a purpose. Every demon plays a role. Satan aims to twist and pervert every system we create and every institution we use to run our country. He does it while blinding every person from following God's ways.

I will reveal a unique perspective, providing insight so you can figure out how to do your part. At the end of this chapter, I will demonstrate the complex plan our mortal enemy is using to twist our own culture and turn it against us.

Let's start with our political system. Most of us already know that our country's political system is an area where deception and lies are the norm. Most of today's presidential campaigns have resorted to slandering and mudslinging. Both political parties pull out all the stops in attempts to make their opponents appear unqualified, unscrupulous, or plain incompetent. Many politicians will say anything to win their campaign, making promises they never intend to keep. Some of these political races have become a circus of smoke and mirrors. The lies and deception are so deep it is impossible to know what to believe.

We have already discussed in previous chapters how wealth, power, and fame gained at any cost are empty of God's eternal blessings. Our political system is an example of how the misuse of power creates corruption. Corrupt power uses injustice to manipulate an unfair advantage. Injustice takes advantage of the voiceless or less fortunate for evil gains. Greed wins at any cost by using imbalanced scales and justifies its intentions by distorting the rules. Our nation seems to possess an insatiable appetite for power and control, which has created an attitude of winning at all costs in business, politics, and our justice system. Our culture operates by its own rules based on what feels good or seems right.

There's a question we should be asking ourselves: What does God think about power-hungry corruption? Ultimately, His opinion is the only one that matters, and our job is to figure out how to address the things that matter to Him.

The answer to that question is: The Lord hates power-hungry deceit. The Bible sums it up in Zechariah 8:16-17, "'These are the things you are to do: Speak the truth to each other, and render true and sound judgment in your courts; do not plot evil against each other, and do not love to swear falsely. I hate all this,' declares the Lord."

This chapter is not a cheap ploy for votes or political party propaganda. Politics are a hot topic. They carry extreme levels of debate and controversy. As a result of the deep controversy, take a moment to pray before we go on. Get yourself centered and focused on hearing God's voice between the lines of every page. Ask the Holy Spirit to open our mind, so He can help us see the condition of our systems, the way He sees them. While doing this, ask the Lord to reveal insightful ways we can become a voice for truth and justice.

Abraham Lincoln said something about America that seems prophetic. "America will never be destroyed from the outside. If we falter and lose our freedoms, it will be because we destroyed ourselves."

On that note, we will jump back into the age-old discussion of church and politics. Sadly, as we stated in an earlier chapter, many Christians will not get involved with our political system. Some everyday Christians believe political systems are secular or just plain evil. Many evangelical leaders believe you should not mix politics

197

and church, and they teach the same from the pulpit. Meanwhile, most pastors try to walk the line of being overly politically correct. Maybe worst of all, many pastors hit it so hard that it totally turns off everybody.

No matter how you personally see it, hopefully we can agree that most of the American church will not engage in our political system to improve our government's policies and laws. There are too many excuses for the church to turn a blind eye to the laws of our land. In the meantime, our government's crooked antics put our entire country under God's judgment. How can we just stick our heads in the sand and hope it all gets better? There is more at stake than we realize.

The U.S. has the most lethal military force in the world, and we are one of the wealthiest countries. Our government uses America's wealth and advanced military forces to influence the entire world by using political manipulation. America uses its wealth to influence other countries by giving it away or making agreements to purchase things from foreign countries. Our wealth is a major source of our political power in the world. When money doesn't work, we simply leverage our military prowess to get our way. Our wealth and military force provide us with an unmatched global political power. Political leverage is used when resolving international issues. Sometimes our government leaders use money or military threats, and other times they send troops.

Washington, DC, is the command center of our government's political and justice systems, including our military force. All these systems are ruled from DC. In addition, when you look at our global influence that is ruled from Washington DC, you can plainly see how DC is the epicenter of the most powerful country on the planet. DC is the perfect place for Satan to control our country. He also uses America's global influence in ways that fulfill his demonic plans to destroy all humanity across the entire planet by turning countries against each other. No wonder DC is home to the most powerful principalities on earth. From there Satan manipulates the world to execute his plans.

Hopefully, you are beginning to see the importance for the church to be God's voice within the halls of our government and political systems. Representing Jesus within our corrupt systems is not a choice if we love Jesus.

The church does not live inside a sterile bubble that exists outside of our society's systems and institutions. If our nation goes down, we all go down with it. We win together and we will all lose together. Winning back our nation involves getting engaged and using our voices to realign our systems with God's ways. Otherwise, it will end in disaster.

The Bible teaches about the consequences of refusing to follow God's ways—curses and death instead of blessings and life, on a global scale. There is more at stake than our own life. The future of our nation rests on each of us taking a collective stand in every area of our lives. It might seem like an overstatement, but unfortunately, it's the truth.

Hopefully by now you are beginning to see the importance of being more assertive with our involvement. Much more could be said about our governmental systems and leaders—how they partner with rich and powerful organizations, keeping their deceitful actions secretive, taking advantage of the powerless and poor, controlling our freedoms of Christianity in ways they should not . . . and the list goes on and on.

The point here is not to list all the reasons to be anti-government or create conspiracy theories. The point is to help us realize that the opportunity to impact the world is much greater than we realize. In fact, we have much more than just an opportunity. Our God-given responsibility is to courageously change our world. At this point, we should be asking ourselves, how can I help? A good start is to connect with our local government's leadership. Here are some simple ways we can get started:

Get involved with your local government meetings to discuss issues that need to be resolved in your city.

Find out what your mayor or governor's hot topics are and get involved to help.

Figure out the important issues your state's attorney general is spending time and resources on.

What are the biggest problems the chief of police is dealing with?

Attend public meetings where your government discusses issues, new laws, etc. Let your voice be heard.

Figure out how you can get involved and you will find out that your local government is trying to address many of the same issues as pastors and ministers are trying to address. What is holding us back from leveraging our local government to advance the kingdom? By getting involved, we will develop relationships with our local government, and you never know where that will lead. You may get the opportunity to share Jesus, utilize their resources and money for kingdom purposes, or just shine the light of Christ. Many government officials will gladly accept help for the issues they are trying to resolve. You can usually find other groups of Christians already teaming up to make changes in your city or state. Team up with folks who have plans in motion. Do not reinvent the wheel if you can partner with those who already have influence.

However, you will need to do some research on your government leaders. It will take time to research, but the information is there. Take the time to assess your city's needs and figure out how you can leverage your government's help. Ask God for favor and an innovative and flexible mindset. Favor is the key ingredient that will open doors for you. The correct mindset will allow you to maximize your opportunities. All the while, you will be rubbing elbows with your city's leaders and shining your light. While you are in the company of these men and women, display deep integrity. Allow your godliness to speak for itself. Your lifestyle of godliness will influence everyone around you.

I have only listed a few ways you can get involved with your local government. You can find many other ways if you spend time doing your homework or getting guidance from others. Before long, you might find yourself running for office or establishing a group of local people who will help address issues that grieve God's heart.

This moment is a critical hour for the church to lead the way toward making right all the things that are wrong. It is the church's obligation to lead the country that God established for us. If we will not, then who will?

They say justice is blind. But we know better than that. An impartial justice system removes racism, discrimination, and socioeconomic status. A fair and just system disregards what we look like, who we know, or how much money we have. An impartial justice system must use equality, impartial laws, and fair judgments. Fame, fortune, and power should not tip the scales of justice. Our justice system has a long history of wrongly accusing people of crimes they never committed. Sending people to prison or death row because of racially driven motives is wrong on so many levels. Most of all, it is a direct sin against God's commands.

Amos 5:15 says, "Hate evil, love good; maintain justice in the courts. Perhaps the Lord God Almighty will have mercy on the remnant of Joseph."

This verse clarifies God's expectations for us to maintain justice. It also shows how we get back into God's graces instead of His judgment. Our systems should protect everyone's civil rights equally. Our unjust systems have created civil upheaval and it has divided our nation.

Our country has a long history of discrimination and racially driven violence. Let's take slavery as an example. Slavery led our country into a civil war. Racism, hatred and ignorance led us further into the tumultuous nineteen hundreds, a time where activists and riots rose up from the injustices of segregation, lynching, and oppression, which finally birthed a civil rights movement. Unfortunately, we still haven't learned from our history of injustices that always lead us to violence and death. You would think we should have learned our lesson by now.

Today, it's still commonplace where men and women are falsely accused and imprisoned. Police brutality and false arrests seem as if they are an everyday occurrence across our nation. You see it on the news or social media way too often. Perhaps the most infamous situations are the Rodney King and George Floyd events.

Rodney King survived a brutal beating by the LAPD after being pulled over for drunk driving. The four officers were caught on tape beating him within an inch of his life. A massive riot broke out in 1992 after the four police officers were acquitted. Thousands of Los Angeles residents turned their city into a war zone. They burned businesses, looted stores, and violently brutalized white people who happened to be driving by the riots.

One of the most recent infamous incidents happened with George Floyd in Minneapolis. He was arrested for buying cigarettes with a counterfeit $20 bill. A few citizens happened to witness the arrest in front of the store and recorded the incident on social media that went viral.

George was held down by several police officers. One police officer forced his knee into George's neck while he lay handcuffed on his stomach. The other three officers held down George and kept the crowd of onlookers at bay, while the witnesses pleaded with the officers for George's life.

George died because the officer's knee cut off his airway. He was murdered on camera, and America watched it all unfold on social media. The incident created a public uproar, and the police officers were immediately fired. They were later convicted of murder. But it was too little too late. Violence immediately erupted. George's murder incited rioting in every major city across the nation. Everyone had had enough. The nation grew tired of corruption and injustice in our legal system. To make it all worse, it happened in the middle of the COVID-19 pandemic when everyone was already on edge. Looting, fires, protests, violence, and civil unrest ensued. It made a bad situation worse.

These despicable incidents of injustice have something in common. Both victims were black men and almost all the police officers were white. Our nation became further divided over an age-old problem.

These examples do not mean every person in our justice/legal system is bad. It simply means our system is broken, and it keeps getting worse. We have an unjust system that discriminates and kills instead of protecting and creating peace. We need systems free from corruption and blind to racial and socioeconomic differences, systems that protect our civil freedoms with justice and biblical integrity at their core.

How do we change corrupt and unjust systems? There is a hint in Psalm 41:1-2. "Blessed are those who have regard for the weak. The Lord delivers them in times of trouble. The Lord protects and preserves them."

We start by standing up for those who do not have a voice. And who are they? They are the cries of 63 million babies silenced by abortion. Victims of rape who watch their perpetrators get off scot-free because nobody believes they were raped against their will.

Child molesters who find ways to beat the system repeatedly. The daily injustices of the wrongfully harassed because of their skin color. And the falsely accused who are too poor or too scared to fight. I'm sure you can think of many more injustices against those whose voices will not be heard.

I don't know how we got here, but I know the founders of America did not have a godless nation in mind when our country was founded. The founders of our country established a nation under God. I read a scripture in Deuteronomy 4:5-8, and it made me wonder if our forefathers read the very same scripture aloud, with great anticipation of establishing a covenant with God to create a God-fearing nation. The scripture says,

> See, I have taught you decrees and laws . . . so that you may follow them in the land you are entering. . . . Observe them carefully, for this will show your wisdom and understanding to the nations, who will hear about all these decrees and say, "Surely this great nation is a wise and understanding people." What other nation is so great as to have their gods near them the way the Lord our God is near us whenever we pray to him? And what other nation is so great as to have such righteous decrees and laws as this body of laws I am setting before you today?

This scripture undoubtedly explains why God made this country so great, to be a beacon unto the world. We are supposed to be a beacon of righteous laws by following God's ways.

I can almost hear God telling us today the words of the scriptures from the remainder of the same chapter in Deuteronomy 4:9-10: "Only be careful, and watch yourselves closely so that you do not forget the things your eyes have seen or let them fade from your heart as long as you live. Teach them to your children and to their children after them. Remember the day you stood before the Lord your God at Horeb, when he said to me, 'Assemble the people before me to hear my words so that they may learn to revere me as long as they live in the land and may teach them to their children.'"

Changing our system will not happen overnight. Change is a big task that seems impossible at first glance. But nothing is impossible for God. We undoubtedly need the hand of God to intervene because we are incapable of changing things without Him. We will fail by doing it our own way. Our biggest and best grandiose plans will never work unless God leads the way. We know one thing is sure—God's plans are sure to win. We can start by asking God for direction, favor, courage, and anointing. Keep in mind that fixing our unjust system is much more important to God than it is to us. His plans involve realigning our ways. Our job is to seek Him and figure out how we can be part of His plan. Then we can rest assured that God's hand will be with us. Psalm 35:10 shows God's plans to fix our broken systems. "You rescue the poor from those too strong for them, the poor and needy from those who wrong them."

We all need to do our part in our own world of influence. Get involved with your local government, federal government, state judicial system, federal judicial system, mayor, governor, or state attorney general, and use your social media presence, etc. Most of all, rely on God's ways because His ways are better than our ways. Begin to ask the Holy Spirit for creative ways to make a dent or at least take a first step.

Whatever you do, never give up. Be ready to go all in. Be ready to fight. Just like Martin Luther King said, "We are determined here in Montgomery to work and fight until justice runs down like water, and righteousness like a mighty stream."

There's another way we can ensure the future of our country and the continued advancement of Christianity. One of the verses in Deuteronomy above provided a hint. We must take a more active role in educating our children to ensure they possess the proper biblical worldview. We must also teach them to take an active role in our society.

According to the Bible, parents have sole responsibility to instill God's ways into their children. The Bible repeatedly instructs parents to teach our children about following God's ways and sharing the things God has done for us. Children must learn God's ways from the very beginning of their lives, which is why it's crucial to teach them young.

Children also repeat what they see. Children will not listen to what we say unless we practice what we preach. They watch what we do. They mimic our behavior. The way we live our life is our children's biggest teacher. Our life's actions speak louder than our words of advice or guidance. Our actions and words must be aligned.

For example, children learn how to love and hate in our homes. They learn racism, discrimination, and bigotry. They also learn to be kind, trusting, and patient.

Deuteronomy 6:6-7 clearly gives us commands about teaching our children God's ways. "These commandments that I give you today are to be on your hearts. Impress them on your children. Talk about them when you sit at home and when you walk along the road, when you lie down and when you get up."

As parents, we must realize our responsibility to raise our children according to God's ways. The best way to lead is by example. And we must be intentional about instilling biblical values.

Unfortunately, our society has grown overly dependent on schools and churches to instill values into our children and prepare them for their future. The parents are responsible, not churches and schools. Most parents are not actively involved beyond ensuring their children's homework is completed. They rely on our education system to teach them everything.

Furthermore, many parents do not take personal responsibility to instill essential biblical values into our children. We need to change that mindset of depending on others to educate our children and being careless about this all-important responsibility. If we take responsibility for our own children and start becoming more effective at home, we will see a new generation with a bright future on its horizon. Once we figure out how to do it at home, perhaps we can create strategies to improve our schools and educational systems.

As it stands today, our educational system plays a strong role in shaping the future of our culture. Since our system is no longer based upon biblical commands and values, its curriculum changes over time. Our educational system adapts to whatever is important to our culture. For example, our schools teach our children to accept the ideal of choosing their sexual orientation, finding their gender identity, and exploring abortion as an option for birth control.

Our universities teach about a godless universe that appeared from thin air. A preposterous theory about a godless creation has convinced masses of people that our planet started life as a molten blob that later produced human beings, evolving from a puddle of sludge. All the while, our higher education systems do everything possible to create new theories attempting to rationalize a universe without God. These godless theories place human ideals at the center of all creation, instead of Jesus.

Our educational system has crossed every line of biblical values, godliness, and righteousness. It now accommodates worship of demonic cults, but it will not tolerate mentioning the name of Jesus. Our children are not allowed to pray in school or study the Bible together. There is undoubtedly a methodical plan to systematically create an anti-biblical worldview that is devoid of Jesus Christ and His commandments. Our educational system is hell bent on destroying our country by spreading the cancer of abominable sin and infecting every child.

Our current system creates an uphill battle, opposing the expansion of God's kingdom. The future is affected by breeding the culture Satan wants our children to live in. His lies propagate across our culture's popular belief systems and instills them into our children's lives, so that they later live out these cancerous beliefs. We must create a new culture for a new future. And our new culture must include teaching our children young, while taking responsibility for instilling godly values and principles in our children. Otherwise, the future of our country does not stand a chance, and we will continue spiraling out of control until our nation finally collapses.

An ideal educational system should prepare our youth for the future by ensuring the advancement of Christianity and the further development of God's kingdom from generation to generation. Our children need to be equipped with the tools they need to create a better nation that improves our culture with every generation.

Unfortunately, Satan has been using our own educational system against us to indoctrinate our youth with perverted lies about creation, marriage, and abortion. He uses our own systems to ensure we establish a foundation that embraces a perverted and twisted culture, a foundation that creates a worse tomorrow and a vicious cycle where our society gets worse.

While many Christians are disengaged, the devil is eating away at our children's faith. The cycle drives many Christian teachers to give up trying to instill biblical values into children within their classrooms because they will lose their jobs if they do. All this happens while the church just sits back and seemingly accepts it all. I often wonder about the level of frustration and discouragement of Christian teachers from lack of our support and involvement.

Here are a few questions to ask ourselves. They might be very hard things to admit, but it is critical we get beyond them into a place of action. Ask God to reveal His will for your life concerning the following questions:

What culture are we allowing our educational system to create? How are we intentionally instilling a biblical worldview into our children? How can we get involved in our local schools or regional educational institution to ensure our voice is heard about the things we want our children exposed to or not exposed to? How will I take responsibility to help improve our educational system? How will I do my part to take a stand?

Now we will switch gears to explore some other things that have a big impact on shaping our culture. The advancement of technology and the endless vehicles of media and information. Our society's technological advancements have provided opportunities to move us forward in many important ways. The ironic thing about our advancements in technology is that we have used them in ways that take us backward in our morality. Instead of growing and strengthening our values, we are experiencing spiritual collapse.

We are constantly bombarded with messages through images, ads, news feeds, and social media from all sorts of outlets. Some communication is specifically targeted at our minds and emotions to influence our thinking, shape our mindsets, and manipulate our actions.

News media sends so many mixed messages. Sometimes they want to increase ratings, so they twist the truth. Other times media outlets are tied to political parties or special interest groups that have power or influence. It has become a game of influence that's controlled by the highest bidder and the loudest voice.

Movies and music also have a way of stirring our emotions and changing our state of mind. They are more than merely a form of entertainment that reflects the state of our culture. They play a strong part in molding and shaping it.

In fact, music has the prophetic power to speak life or sooth our souls. Go read my book titled *Rising Soundz: From Pain to Purpose* if you want to learn more about how music impacts our souls and the spiritual world around us.

Of course, movies and music are not bad within themselves. Satan uses them as tools to pervert God's ways with evil intentions. Our society is shaped by the things we hear and see on television, internet, and social media. They create new cultural norms, pushing the boundaries of acceptability, some for the better and some for the worse. The new boundaries have transformed over the past few years into something unexpected. Rappers talk about killing, raping, robbing, and selling drugs. Other genres of music talk about suicide, cheating on your spouse and demonic worship. There are popular singers like Beyoncé who perform on stage shaking every part of her body, while wearing the skimpiest outfits, leaving nothing to the imagination.

Many female artists have resorted to using sensuality for fame and popularity. Their decision makes things worse for women everywhere. The new standard of sexual antics is degrading and dehumanizing because it sends a perverse message that women cannot make it on their talent or intelligence alone. I often wonder what women from the past, who spent their entire lives fighting tirelessly for a woman's right to vote in our country, would say. In my opinion, it is a disgusting display that sets women back a hundred years.

Not all women have resorted to selling sexuality for fame. Some women have used their fame to take a stand. A very successful tennis player named Serena Williams used her popularity to leverage women's equality in tennis. Serena and her sister Venus crashed onto the scene in women's professional tennis in the mid-nineties. These two African American girls grew up in Compton, California. Being women of color, they began their professional careers with lots of strikes against them, in both the public's eye and the traditions of tennis. A large part of the public and media initially saw them as a couple of black girls from the ghetto who dishonored the game because of their inner-city background, dark skin color, and infamous hair beads. Nobody expected much from these little girls.

God had a different plan for their lives. Serena later became the most dominant and decorated athlete ever seen in tennis—man or woman. Serena and her sister dominated the singles Grand Slam tournaments with back-to-back wins. Their dominance did not stop there. When they played together as a team, no other team in the world stood a chance. The Williams sisters remained unbeaten in Grand Slam doubles finals with a 14-0 record. Total domination. Even that phrase does not do justice to their game-changing determination and inner strength.

Serena's list of accomplishments goes on and on, including four Olympic gold medals. Her career went on to overshadow her older sister's. In 2017, she became the only woman on the Forbes list of the 100 highest paid athletes. She was also named Sportsperson of the Year by *Sports Illustrated* magazine in December 2015. Serena's awards and groundbreaking accolades are unmatched in almost every sport.

Serena's accomplishments on the court were only part of her most significant achievements. She displayed great courage and perseverance when breaking down barriers of race, gender, and socioeconomic background. Serena displayed pride for who she is and where she came from. She showed women everywhere you could be a dark-skinned woman with normal body proportions while never comprising your integrity. She stood proud and confident. She was a game changer who changed the culture.

During the height of her career, Serena put her fame and popularity on the line for women's equality. She took a stand for equal pay in women's tennis. The governing bodies in tennis did not recognize women's contributions to the sport. The governing organizations in tennis refused to pay female tournament winners the same as men. Their leadership claimed women's contributions were less significant than men's contributions.

Serena knew better. Her major endorsements eclipsed everyone else's, even the men's. She was well aware of the high television ratings she brought to the table. Serena decided to put it all on the line by confronting the governing bodies and their leaders. She was ready to pull out of a big tournament if they didn't pay women the same as men. The tournament leaders had no choice but to concede to the tremendous pressure that her popularity demanded. Serena won a fight that several women in tennis had fought for decades. She singlehandedly changed the game of tennis forever.

A young African American girl from the inner city of Compton, California, broke down barriers that transcended the game of tennis on an international scale. Her voice sent a message to every sport. Serena's determination and willingness to put her career on the line inspired little girls all over the world. Her courage and willingness to take a stand gave women the confidence to dream beyond their environment and to break free of the past shackles of society's mindset of bigotry and inferiority.

Serena received several awards for her activism. She was listed among the thirty-five "Most remarkable and beautiful black women" in the world by *Essence* magazine. And the President of NAACP recognized the Williams sisters with their most prestigious Image Award.

I love this story. It shows the power of God. The Williams sisters grew up in the ghettos of Compton, California. Most people would not expect such bright shining stars to come out of such a dark and violent city. In fact, I'm sure the two sisters never could've dreamed how big their impact would be on sports and women everywhere. Look what God did with their lives and look how they used their popularity and fame to change their part of the world. Serena's character shined the brightest when it counted most. That type of character is earned and forged in hard times. I believe that her background prepared her with courage and tenacity.

This story proves that anyone can have a big impact on our society. God loves to turn our bad situations into something good. He uses the most unlikely people to do the most amazing things.

This is only one of many stories of people who made a difference. There are several famous actors and artists who took a stand to change their industry by advancing Christianity.

Kirk Cameron was a child star who later started producing and self-funding some of the most impactful Christian movies ever created. And Mel Gibson did the same with the most powerful movie about Jesus in *The Passion of the Christ*.

You may not have the same level of popularity or fame at this point in your life. However, your contributions to our society are just as important. You can make a difference in your part of the world.

Do you have some sort of influence, popularity, or fame? Perhaps you have a big social media following, run a podcast, or influence emerging leaders. Ask the Lord to give you a heart for the things that grieve His Spirit and the courage to put it all on the line. Dare to make a difference beyond your wildest dreams.

Martin Luther King made a powerful statement about taking a stand. "There comes a time when one must take a position that is neither safe nor politic nor popular, but he must take it because his conscience tells him it is right."

The previous chapters and sections in this book are meant to take you on a journey of how we arrived at this place in our nation. When you put the pieces together, it should be plain to see that Satan has been methodically removing God from every corner of our country. There is a method to Satan's plans for destroying our nation. He has created a downward spiraling cycle by using the very institutions we created to run our country. Plainly stated, we have allowed Satan to use our own systems against us.

Now I'll connect the dots to reveal how Satan uses our entire culture against us. You will see how the individual parts create a complex system that is fed by our greed and personal pursuit for power, fame, and wealth. Let's jump in.

First, Satan leads our heart astray. He uses methods like fatherlessness to destroy families, creating broken homes and broken people. The brokenness creates a root that grows sin in our lives. Our hearts become corrupt and our ways become perverted, so everything we touch becomes corrupt.

Then our corrupt and perverted ways spill over into the way we do business. Cheating, stealing, and lying become the norm in our shrewd business practices. Sinful business dealings are now considered acceptable and good. Big businesses use their wealth to keep pushing the lines of ethics by partnering with our government to manipulate our laws in ways that allow businesses to keep bending the rules. Greed digs its claws into our government leaders and further corrupts them since they are influenced by power and votes.

Our corrupt hearts have allowed our political system to be reduced to political games with an agenda of wealth and power at their core. Big business and big government have become a way to fill an ever-growing appetite for wealth and power.

Satan also uses factions or big groups of people to further influence our laws with the threat of withholding votes for political parties. These factions force the creation of new laws so things such as drugs, abortion, and other harmful things remain legalized. Our government system is reduced to political maneuvering that disregards doing good for the common people. The outcome of these political games is a path of destruction. Our "evolving" laws create new values that directly contradict God's ways, taking our society further and further away from God. We have replaced blessings with curses by inventing new ways to sin.

As a result, we inject our twisted ways into our legal/judicial systems. Legalizing our godless ways allow us to use our systems to justify our actions and enforce our demented ways. The new laws make the general public think it's acceptable to sin against God. Our laws are steeped in sin, and they weave our wicked ways into the fabric of our culture.

These new laws are constantly fed into our educational system, where they are taught to our children as acceptable. Our newly devised norms are established as a new standard of beliefs and values. Education is a way to ensure tomorrow's leaders are indoctrinated with an anti-biblical viewpoint. This locks that viewpoint into place as a new foundation. Then Satan can move forward, continuing to build more lies, death, and destruction on top of a foul foundation.

There's a final piece to the diabolical puzzle. Satan influences our music, movies, news outlets, and social media to keep pushing us further and further past the lines of godly justice, righteousness, and holiness. Our news outlets spew lies and twist the truth for ratings, while music and movies constantly push the boundaries of acceptability. We do the same thing with our personal social media. It has become an illusion where we project a deceptive lifestyle of popularity, wealth, or success. Everybody wants to sound like the smartest person, and nobody wants to be the most humble and teachable person.

Each cultural element works together to create an organized system—a vicious cycle that pushes us further away from God and somehow creates the deception of acceptability. The cycle has created a culture where perverted lifestyles are celebrated and Christian lifestyles are intolerable.

Satan is using each element from our culture to weave a sticky web. His army is playing a masterful level of chess, while we have become trapped in our own web of selfishness. Every move they make targets our King, to remove Him from the board. That's exactly what we are allowing when the church disengages and chooses to avoid involvement. Satan changed the rules by turning the tables on us, and our world is upside down.

We should not be surprised about each generation getting worse. We have blindly allowed our own institutions to create a vicious cycle that is bringing curses upon our families and our nation—a cycle that we must disrupt and turn around very soon before it's too late. As I stated earlier, getting involved is not an option. Realigning our culture is an obligation.

God's judgment is on our land, and His attempts to give us a wake-up call do not seem to be getting past our stubbornness and selfishness. We need a new cycle that perpetuates godly values and follows God's ways, a cycle that continuously grows our understanding of God's ways and deepens our commitment to them. We need to, as a people, get better and better, every generation, in our commitment and obedience to God's instructions.

These words from Jeremiah 7:2-7 ring true for us at this moment: "Hear the word of the Lord, all you people [of America]. . . . Reform your ways and your actions, and I will let you live in this place . . . if you really change your ways and your actions and deal with each other justly, if you do not oppress the foreigner, the fatherless or the widow and do not shed innocent blood in this place, and if you do not follow other gods to your own harm, then I will let you live in this place, in the land I gave your ancestors for ever and ever."

One thing is certain: Our nation's fall is inevitable if things do not change. Although I am personally convinced the gospel of Jesus

Christ will flourish if our nation crumbles, we still cannot sit back and watch our nation slip through God's hand of judgment. Who is going to help our nation turn around? How will we break the cycle?

You should know the answer by now! God's church is the answer, the body of Christ, believers who love Jesus, like you and me. This is the very reason Jesus created His church . . . to turn our world toward Him. We must assume responsibility and take a stand—now.

The church has relinquished its voice, and now we must take a stand to become the conscience of America once again. We are the head and not the tail. We must step away from our political position of playing it safe and accept the church's role as the leader of America's soul.

Martin Luther King wrote, "The church has been an echo rather than a voice, a taillight behind the Supreme Court and other secular agencies, rather than a headlight guiding men progressively and decisively to higher levels of understanding."

11

Where's God's Church?

Fear and chaos have gripped our nation. Things appear to be getting worse in our country and throughout the world, especially after COVID-19 hit. It changed everything. As a pastor and apostolic leader, one of the biggest questions I kept hearing across the country was, Where is the church? In this chapter, we are going to explore this question deeper than we did in the previous chapters. We will look at how the church is impacting our entire culture, where God is taking the church and how we can do our part to strengthen the body of Christ.

Before we dive into answering questions about the church, I need to establish a critical truth. We need to get our minds right about God's church because we often fail to see the church in the correct light for many reasons. Some people have been hurt by the church.

Others see the church as condemning, money hungry, or out of touch with the world's broken reality. Some people feel as if they need to put on a figurative mask to appear to have it all together, while others see the church as a list of rules that impose unrealistic expectations. Maybe the most damaging reputation of all is that many people believe church is something you attend on Sundays—a mindset many American Christians have today.

Our perspective of the church must be realigned with the eyes of God. If our perspective of the church is distorted, it will create dysfunction within the church. The results will be frustration, disappointment, and hurt. These pains of reality exist within church members, church leaders, and even people who have never set foot in a church building. But the reality is that Jesus created the church to be the answer for everything that troubles the world. Jesus invented the church to be a divine family of Jesus followers who carry His presence into the darkest places.

There are so many people who talk harshly about God's church. Social media is out of control with the hateful posts and comments against Jesus followers. Many believers inside the church mistreat each other, criticizing local churches, slandering pastors or other ministers, and talking as if they know more than everyone else. We even hear Christians talk about how the church should be managed and structured, or what goals it should accomplish, which is nothing more than a bunch of opinions and personal ideals that lead to shallow results. A feeble attempt to sound smart or appear to know more than everyone else.

Some Christians and ministers go as far as causing division and destruction within the church, as if they own it, growing their own ministries from chaos. Division is a result from selfishness and ignorance, rooted in pride and insecurities. The fact is, the church is holy, and it is the most important thing to God in the entire universe. The church is so important to God, He refers to it as the bride of Christ. Establishing His bride cost Jesus His lifeblood.

The Bible is clear about Jesus as the head of the church. However, Jesus does much more than merely lead the church. He owns it. We, as His church body, are part of His very being. Nobody has the right to slander her, divide her, or cause harm to her, nor should we support such things. Treat the bride of Christ with care

233

and caution, or we could find ourselves on the wrong end of God's judgment.

Our role within the church is to protect her, build her, and strengthen her according to Jesus' commands. One of our life's purposes is to strive toward loving her the way Jesus does. She is Jesus' crown jewel and we are privileged to serve her.

It's imperative to start this chapter with the correct perspective and attitude about Jesus' church. To do that, we must see her the way Jesus does. The best way I know how is through Scripture. We will use scripture from Revelation 5 because it provides a perspective from heaven's viewpoint.

Revelation 5 paints an amazing picture of the church. I'll attempt to convey the picture I see in this scripture. You definitely need to study the chapter for yourself. I'm sure the Holy Spirit will reveal deeper truths than I'm capable of expressing. God's Word has a way of revealing itself in unique ways, especially when we meditate on it for ourselves. The Holy Spirit will paint a more vivid picture than my meager vocabulary can describe.

The book of Revelation is written by John. The Lord took John into heaven to see a perspective of the world from heaven's vantagepoint. Here he heard God's voice, spoke to angelic beings, and witnessed God's future plans poured out onto mankind. Chapter 5 is such an important moment in Revelation because it's a prelude to the Lord breaking open the seven seals of a great scroll. Let's dive in.

Angelic beings surrounded God's throne while He held a great scroll, and majestic hosts of heaven waited in anticipation of God's purposes and plans pouring out onto the earth. Heaven seemed to pause when God could not find anyone worthy to open the great scroll.

John begins weeping over the seemingly tragic moment. Suddenly, the Lamb of God appears and takes the scroll. The Lamb, looking as if it had been slain, is Jesus. As Jesus takes the scroll, a celebration breaks out in heaven because of the new covenant, created at the cost of Jesus' blood. Thousands upon thousands of heavenly hosts break out into a new song. The song's lyrics are recorded in Revelation 5:9-10 and describe the monumental moment in history when Jesus sacrificed Himself at the cross.

"You are worthy to take the scroll and to open its seals, because you were slain, and with your blood you purchased for God persons from every tribe and language and people and nation. You have made them to be a kingdom and priests to serve our God, and they will reign on the earth."

God's words are true, and they are the basis for all creation. In this critical moment, before the great seals are opened, we see the new family Jesus created and purchased with His blood. The text describes a divine family that's redeemed by Jesus' death and resurrection. His blood purchased people of every color, language, ethnicity, and nation. God's grace reaches all peoples from all places. Nobody is out of God's reach. No soul is too dark or hidden from His hand. This text refers to a new, divine family that He named the ecclesia (or the church) gathered from every people on earth. His new family will inherit God's kingdom through the Lamb's blood. Followers of Jesus become sons and daughters of the one and only Creator of the universe.

Psalm 68:6 says, "God sets the lonely in[to] families, He leads out the prisoners with singing."

Immediately following Revelation 5, we read about the seven seals of God's judgment opened. Why does the Bible describe the church's birth before the seven seals are opened? There's only one answer. Jesus created the church to be a beacon of light for a fallen world. We carry the only divine power capable of irradicating the cancer of sin that plagues the hearts of mankind. If you're not paying attention, as you read the book of Revelation, you will miss the beauty of the solution He created before the first seal of judgement was opened. As He opens the seven seals, it's plain to see they are meant to drive mankind into His church, where we possess the answer for all that troubles our world.

Revelation 5:14 concludes the chapter with a heavenly celebration over God's new family: "The four living creatures said, 'Amen,' and the elders fell down and worshiped."

Heaven bears witness to the birth of a new hope. Jesus Christ established a new age for the future of mankind.

237

Now we will briefly look at how the church was born, from a different viewpoint. The events in Acts 2 record how the church was born on earth. The Bible describes it happening on the day of Pentecost when Jesus breathed life into her. Try to imagine how the events described in Revelation 5 manifested on earth during the day of Pentecost.

Read what Jesus said in Acts 1:6-7 before He thrust the church into the world. He commanded every follower to realign the world's wicked ways before breaking open the first seal. "Then they gathered around him (Jesus) and asked him, 'Lord, are you at this time going to restore the kingdom to Israel?' He said to them: 'It is not for you to know the times or dates the Father has set by his own authority. But you will receive power when the Holy Spirit comes on you; and you will be my witnesses in Jerusalem, and in all Judea and Samaria, and to the ends of the earth.'"

Jesus commanded all believers to change the world before He thrust His church into the world. His commands gave us power and authority to get the job done. Then He breathed life into the church in Acts 2:1-2: "When the day of Pentecost came, they were all together in one place. Suddenly a sound like the blowing of a violent wind came from heaven and filled the whole house."

God's breath brings life. The Bible says God created Adam and breathed the breath of life into him, and man became a living being (Genesis 2:7). God created mankind on the earth with His life-giving breath. Jesus breathed the same breath of life into the church and a new divine family was born on earth. Jesus shed His blood so we can become carriers of His kingdom and accomplish His purposes on earth.

I said all of those things to say this: John witnessed a spectacular event in heaven, and on the day of Pentecost God's will was witnessed on earth. After the church was born, the world was never the same. Jesus created His church to offer the world a new beginning, a new future, and a new life.

As the Lord continues to break open the seven seals, His church carries the life-giving presence of the Holy Spirit. The church was designed to hold the greatest mysteries of God, which is the life-giving love of Jesus. If sin is a cancer, God's church is the answer.

Hopefully, we are seeing the role of God's church in the world from the proper perspective. A proper perspective will allow us to see some of the challenges the church faces today, which can feel never-ending to pastors.

Their leadership teams are constantly navigating through difficulties such as, growing their church (numerically and spiritually), sermons being too deep or too shallow, motivating the congregation to evangelize on their own and read and pray daily. All the while, they're dealing with issues such as, deciding on types of worship music, handling children's ministries and the unrealistic pressures from their own congregation to do more and be more.

The issues happening in our world add more challenges to this daunting list, as if building the church wasn't already hard enough. Issues of today are more difficult than ever, causing deeper levels of brokenness. They range from legalized marijuana, same sex marriages, racial unrest, abortion, human trafficking, COVID-19, and the effects of our appetite for greed and power, all of which are downright destructive. The list goes on and on, seemingly getting worse every year.

Although the list of challenges is long and heavy, God's Spirit will overcome. The Holy Spirit is already moving within the hearts of people from the most unlikely and hopeless places. Jesus is taking prostitutes and turning them into godly mothers and transforming adulterers into godly fathers. He is replacing depression with courage and confidence to fulfill God-given purposes. The hopeless and oppressed are now overcomers and accomplished. God's hand is taking the blind and using them as a beacon of light.

A move of God is happening in places we have never seen in America before. Kingdom opportunities exist at every turn to shine Jesus' light into the darkest depths of our cities and corrupt culture. Jesus called us to be more than representatives of Him. Our responsibility to influence and lead the way is greater than merely wearing Christian t-shirts or creating controversial posts on social media. Most of us will never change our culture if those are our main tools to advance God's kingdom. We are the hands and voice of Jesus Christ, the one and only true God of all things, and He commissioned us to take the lead.

The truth is, we have weaknesses within the American church that need to be realigned with Jesus' expectations. While many things appear to be changing for the worse in our world, the American church seems to be losing ground on many levels. The biggest tragedy is that Jesus created the church to change the world. But overall, the world is affecting the church more than the church is affecting our world.

This became most apparent when COVID-19 turned our world upside down. It touched down like a tornado and left a path of destruction in its wake. The Corona virus affected everybody, and it changed everything for the entire world. Sadly, most of the church did not know how to react. They were ill-prepared, at best. At worst, many pastors did not see a need to change, and they prayed for things to get back to *normal*. But things will never be *normal* again. Lord forbid we ever get back to some form of comfortable normality. I personally hope we never become comfortable with building an anemic church void of a commitment to Jesus and His mission.

I pray the Lord leads us to a place where we are stretched and challenged to dedicate our lives to Him and His mission. Lead us, Lord, into a deeper love that gives everything we have during our short time on earth.

Our desire to remain comfortable has cost us dearly. The way COVID crippled our churches was a blatant example of our inability to adapt and our unwillingness to react swiftly and decisively. Many churches were financially devastated. Countless churches were incapable of taking advantage of hardships to help their communities in ways that evangelize because they were too focused on maintaining salaries and ownership of their buildings, as if it were the only thing that made them viable. Sadly, too many local churches stopped being the church and strictly went into survival mode, all while God was pushing us to stop attending church and start being the church.

There's irony in it all. Pastors have always been pushing their congregations to engage in God's Word and His mission, striving toward a higher percentage of their congregation to dedicate their lives to God's teaching and growing the kingdom. In fact, most pastors try to fit those two subjects into every sermon, every Sunday. For the most part, it seems to fall on deaf ears. I personally used to pray endlessly for my church to grow in these areas, spending countless hours teaching my congregation about every believer's responsibility to build God's kingdom and lean into Jesus.

Then the Lord spoke to me. He made it crystal clear that I was not leading the church in a way that's obedient to His requirements. You see, as the senior pastor, everything centers on one person. The pastor does most of the preaching, makes the most important decisions, leads the overall ministries, and is central to each local church. As pastors, we teach one way of advancing God's kingdom, but the congregation sees something different.

From the congregation's perspective, church is something we attend instead of who we are. We attend a Sunday service and sit in comfortable chairs watching the big stage, with feelings of anticipation about what God has in store for us that day. Most of us read a few verses from the Bible during the week, but we expect the pastor to primarily feed our soul on Sundays. Tragically, our prayer life typically consists of a laundry list of needs we give to God, rarely getting into God's presence. Maybe we listen to some Christian music throughout the week, especially when we feel down. We might even volunteer our time at church to support various needs or ministries.

As Sunday service begins, we look forward to finally worshipping God in an atmosphere where we can feel His presence because we think church is the only place we can do that. We watch staff members conduct the services, each with various responsibilities. Then the pastor gives some teaching that touches an emotional chord in our soul or challenges us to make a change. Most of the time, we experience an emotional moment that fades as we leave the building and return to our normal lives. Often times, we forget the teaching and we treat commitments we made at church like a New Year's resolution. They quickly fade out and fall by the wayside.

We have created a pastor-centric church where one person is the most important person in the church. The leaders of the church do most of the work while the majority attend and watch, only engaging internally with an occasional shout of amen or hallelujah. Our traditional model we follow every Sunday sets an example that only a few select people have a responsibility to lead anything, while the rest of us do our part by throwing a few dollars in the donation basket. Advancing the kingdom has been resorted to trying to do good, treat people right and, advance God's kingdom by contributing our money to those few people who are called to advance God's kingdom. While those things are not bad, they certainly fail to reflect the entirety of Jesus' commands for every believer who calls themselves a Christian. Jesus has more in mind for His church body and He requires more from us.

Although leadership is vitally important, I see a very different way of leading within the first century church. Church leadership was comprised of teams. Teams of leaders were responsible for making various decision to lead and direct the church. For example, the church elders sent Paul and Barnabas on various missions. Paul led teams into unreached cities and countries to establish new works and grow the kingdom. The books of Timothy and Titus show us that Paul established a team of elders to lead the church for each city. Within those books, we also see that apostles also addressed problems amongst the corporate church body in large regions. Acts 15 provides a great example where James gathered an entire council to make critical decisions about the gentile church in other countries.

The book of Acts also shows numerous examples of the entire church engaged growing and maturing the church, engaged with their communities and culture. Each person helped each other and their communities to meet their financial needs. Everyone played a part in making the church an integral part of its community. The early church never thought of itself as a service they attended. In fact, Jesus never describes it that way. Sadly, God's church has been distilled down to something we attend rather than defining who we are. God's church should define our culture, not the other way around.

Some of us already know about these things, but we may not be following them in terms of the way we lead or build. For those who are unfamiliar with the early church and how it operated, you will need to study it for yourself. Again, this book is only meant to launch you into deeper biblical study and meditation to seek God's will. My words should not change the course of your kingdom building, without first confirming with the Bible and His Spirit. You need to hear from the Holy Spirit and follow His will. Don't believe everything you hear until you confirm its alignment with God's Word.

When you dive deeper into study, you will discover men and women who were engaged in telling people about Jesus, maturing the church, and growing the kingdom. Early Christians seemed to do it as part of their everyday lives. As you study, new questions will start to arise, like: Why were early Christians so dedicated to Jesus and His kingdom compared to the American church? Why isn't the entire congregation reading, praying, helping each other, and building God's kingdom?

As a pastor, I used to ask myself these questions repeatedly, spending countless hours praying, seeking, and hoping. As a minister, church leader or minister you have undoubtedly asked yourself the very same questions, praying the very same things.

When I look back at it now, I can see the answer more clearly. The American church has created a model instead of creating a divine family. A model with a few doing most of the work. While we speak about teamwork, it really isn't set up that way. A few are responsible for the many, while the majority sit on the sidelines never getting involved with anything. Instead of focusing on developing deep relationships with one another, learning and following God's Word together, helping each other grow, we focus on programs, bathrooms, and comfortable chairs.

In the background, leadership is working on things like logos, branding, marketing, and ways to entice people to walk in the doors. Part of our goals are often focused on buying bigger buildings, better facilities, and a bigger sound system, where one person talks, and everyone else listens. In short, our local churches are not functioning like the divine family described in Revelation 5 because congregations follow what they see, not what they are told.

Hopefully we have answered some of the question about why the American church has so many gaps in it.

Our leader-centric way of building God's kingdom is not set up as a family of equal responsibilities, where everyone is involved. We could be setting up networks of home fellowship and home churches where every Christian is engaged and responsible for expanding and growing the kingdom. Instead, leaders are overprotective and paranoid about losing members, losing their position, or losing income. Insecurities and clever ideas often override Jesus' expectations for the type of church He requires.

To put it plainly, we are not giving Jesus the type of church He requires from us. We have created a different version, mostly to make it more palatable for the world to swallow. We spend more time with logos, branding, buildings, and big events than we do trying to give Jesus the type of church He requires.

My statements may come across as disrespectful or dishonoring. However, that is so far from the truth. My intent is to help the church see Jesus' expectations differently. I am not diminishing the foundation established by generations of pastors and ministers throughout the history of our great nation. Just the opposite. I honor their work and I feel privileged to reap the fruit of their labor. In fact, I have intentionally sought out mentors and spiritual parents who have contributed to the kingdom for decades. I am honored to have such committed and dedicated spiritual parents, and I stand on the backs of such dedicated leaders.

Nonetheless, I would be negligent if I do anything less than stand up to strengthen the body of Christ. As a pastor, I asked Jesus for forgiveness when He revealed His requirements in a better light. He showed me the gaps and weaknesses, compared to what we read in the Bible. At that time, I began to see where and how we could strengthen her.

It's our job to strengthen the church that previous generations have built. If we want the church to start engaging in God's Word and His mission, we must start building God's kingdom accordingly. We need to do things differently before we can expect more effective results.

The days of creating a pastor-centric church where the staff do most of the work must end. We must create a Jesus-centric church, where every believer is involved with building, strengthening, and loving. A new and more effective church is needed to turn around our society. One that creates multitudes of leaders who are engaged with God's Word and His mission. We need a church that can survive any pandemic or extreme persecution.

I know this is easier said than done. I do not claim to have all the answers, but I do know that it will only happen through believers who are committed to following God's Word in the way we live and the way we lead. The Holy Spirit will show us how and provide opportunities if we have the courage to follow.

Our grandiose visions and ministry goals should never be to preach in front of multitudes where we are the center of attention. The results of such a church have already proven incapable of simple things like a relationship with Jesus, faithfulness, and endurance— producing a hollow church void of God's power that crumbles when the wind of adversity blows.

I am by no means saying that we have no need for pastors. I personally pastored a few local churches for many years. I am merely saying we must lead the church where we are not the center of attention. As leaders, we need to reevaluate Jesus' expectations for us to grow and mature His church. He expects every single follower to be dependent upon Him, His presence, and His Word. We are supposed to live it out together. God's church should be actively engaged in his or her world with a missionary mindset, bathed in our prayers. I'm aware that all these things have been said before and most pastors teach them weekly. However, the way we do things in our buildings sends a different message and creates a different church. We are not practicing what we preach. Our obedience leading and growing the church must match our sermons.

Jesus requires us to create a strong church with depth of character, purpose, and meaningful love. That means a renewed church that multiplies leaders instead of trying to add followers. Kingdom math multiplies leaders, while man's math adds and subtracts followers. When the church arrives at higher place of maturity and effectiveness, the entire world will see God's grace and experience His healing power.

The Holy Spirit used the Corona virus to strengthen the body of Christ while simultaneously revealing many of its weaknesses. Although Satan used the virus to cause mass chaos, the Holy Spirit used it to show us some fundamental values that we lack. The Lord reprioritized our lives to put Him first. We were forced to create deeper relationships within our homes and amongst our kingdom family. We yearned for corporate worship, and we cherished moments when we were able to spend quality time with our kingdom family. The Lord even gave us some long-needed sabbaths across the entire land. God always finds a way to turn the tables on Satan, every time. God always uses Satan's evil intentions to produce good things.

God is obviously taking drastic measures to seize the world's attention to start depending on Him. Unfortunately, much of the world is moving further away from Jesus and His ways. Our world needs to hear His message of hope and healing. Jesus' church must bring healing to our broken world.

Sadly, most of the church is still trying to find new ways to do the same old things within the confines of our buildings and programs. Our innovation has fallen short. Meanwhile, we lack the core values that made the first century church an unstoppable force. We lack the values they lived by and most of all, the values they died for.

The tumultuous times during COVID revealed gaping holes in the church and everyone was forced to do things differently. While pastors were forced to rethink kingdom building, weaknesses in the church became apparent. Churches across the country began losing members. The dwindling tithes made things worse. Pastors watched their members' faith fall apart under the pressures of uncertain times, further revealing weaknesses in the church body, and we saw its faith fail. Faithfulness faltered and commitment to Jesus crumbled.

After watching the church flounder, there's little doubt we need to make radical changes to the way we are building the body of Christ. It became apparent that the church we created is unable to adequately withstand adversity. Instead of flourishing during adversity, much of the church began to crumble.

One thing needs to be said: COVID was not a surprise to God. He knew that chaos would follow. In fact, the Holy Spirit has been maturing the church during the past few decades, building up the church in areas we have lacked, as if He is creating a fuller expression of His bride. We seem to be living in a moment in church history when the Holy Spirit is constructing the final pieces as a body. A new era has arrived where God's hand completes the church in a fullness our nation has never seen—an expression of the church capable of fulfilling our great nation's destiny to become a beacon of light unto the world.

How do we build going forward? I don't have all the answers, but I do know a couple of things for sure. Bringing the old ways into the new era won't work the way it used to. We need to redefine *what* we are building before we strategize *how* we will build. In other words, the results of our kingdom building are much more important than the processes we use to get there. As we embark on this new journey, we won't be able to rely on our own strength or our extensive experience. We will only have the Lord to rely upon.

Here are some common misconceptions and important elements about the church that will help us move forward together.

Misconceptions about God's church

- Many people think services should only be held in buildings, homes, coffee shops, inside, outside, etc. God's church is not contingent upon meetings. It should only be contingent upon meaningful relationships.

- Judging God's church is not our place. Don't despise God's church with judgmental criticism, regardless of our thoughts about her level of maturity, immaturity, commitment to Christ, the way *they* do church, etc.

- God alone will mold the church as He sees fit. Growing the church is Jesus' responsibility. He created the church, and He alone has the authority to determine how He wants to grow it. Our job is to remain teachable, while following His leading.

Important elements the church should value

- Jesus created a divine family. Church is not a meeting or event that happens on Sundays. It is a dynamic body of believers, who are Holy Spirit-filled, Jesus-loving servants with high obedience who make a united effort to fulfill God's command to create disciples *and* teach nations to follow His ways.

- Become intentional about building intimate relationships, which are foundational for the kingdom.

- Spend our time and money serving others. Inject ourselves into people's lives.

- Commit ourselves to obedience in leading and growing the church according to God's ways, making course corrections along the way as our understanding of Scripture grows.

Our personal commitment to Christ and His commands must be expressed through a deep devotion to prayer, a growing appetite for His Word, and relational fellowship with our fellow believers. Strive daily to stretch our faith and set an example of our commitment to Christ by displaying relentless love through obedient acts of forgiveness, humility, and unhindered giving.

Local churches with lots of members face the biggest challenge being obedient to Jesus' commands about building a relational church. However, each of us are accountable to God for the kingdom we produce for Him. In other words, there's no room for disobedience. Build exactly what He's asking and figure out ways to do it. Begin by seeking God's voice and have the courage to follow His lead.

Look at Scripture closely in the New Testament and you will come closer to the conclusion that we absolutely need each other much more than we realize. Jesus created the church with unique individual qualities that shine brightest when we work together. I

believe there is deeper meaning to Jesus' words of unity in John

17:20-23, where He prayed,

> My prayer is not for them alone. I pray also for those who will believe
> in me through their message, that all of them may be one, Father, just
> as you are in me and I am in you. May they also be in us so that the
> world may believe that you have sent me. I have given them the glory
> that you gave me, that they may be one as we are one—I in them and
> you in me, so that they may be brought to complete unity. Then the
> world will know that you sent me and have loved them even as you
> have loved me.

There is no doubt this scripture contains a deeper meaning than

meets the eye about unity within the church body. The biggest

question is, How can we realign today's church with Jesus'

expectations? How do we migrate into a harmonious body of

believers? Are we capable of loving Jesus and loving each other to

such a degree that we are willing to put our own agendas aside and

embrace our differences? Can we step up to this God moment and

take full advantage of our world's condition by maturing to the

fullness of Christ in unity, the way Jesus is one with the Father? This

part rests squarely on our shoulders. However, there is no doubt in

my mind that the Holy Spirit will orchestrate our efforts if we put

259

our hearts and all our strength toward becoming a family who relies on each other.

Prophets have been declaring for a few years that we have entered a new era, an era where the church body must step into its role of global responsibility. We can no longer merely attend church. We must begin to *be* the church and function as a church body. The days of filling seats must end. That type of church is shallow, lacks power, and is void of deep faith. We need a restart, and COVID gave us that opportunity. Now we can begin again and start learning how to create a church that will live and die by biblical values that change our culture.

None of us knows how the church will look when God is done reshaping us, but one thing is clear: We need to start now. We must become a smarter church and a more dynamic church that learns as we go . . . that gets better as we move forward. Continuously implementing God's inspired revelation from His word and correcting our course, learning from each other along the way, as we all learn how to live out our growing understanding of how the church is supposed to respond to our world's epidemic of sin.

How do we learn to function more effectively as a whole? We just go forward without having all the answers! Planning and strategizing are important, but we cannot allow a lack of extensive planning and strategizing to paralyze our movement. We can trust the Holy Spirit to continue revealing to us these mysteries that are buried in Scripture. Jesus is building His church and He knows what He is doing. Realigning the church is His job. But it will take our trust and a big step of faith. Then we can fulfill His mission by utilizing each part of the body of Christ.

Advancing Christianity goes beyond telling people about Jesus. Although sharing Jesus is a staple, there is much more to it. Advancing Christianity means we are evolving as individuals, as a global church body, and as a nation, but in a different way than evolution is currently taught. Evolving as individuals means continuous growth in our individual commitment and love for Jesus. Evolving as a nation means maturing as a united body of believers, while uncovering truths that allow us to instill His ways into every corner of our society.

Notice how I wove together evolution of the church body with our nation's spiritual maturity. The only way our nation will become spiritually healthy, in God's eyes, is if the church body is continuously evolving into a fuller expression of Jesus' expectations. In other words, changing our old ways to become obedient to everything we see in the Bible. We should simply read and apply, forgoing our old ways that have become tradition rather than commands from Jesus.

There must be generational growth in all these things, a different sort of evolution—one that ensures we establish an ever-growing foundation that each generation builds upon. We need to know the biblical values and morals of the previous generations that they lived and died by. How did their values and morals play a part in driving them to stand up against the extreme adversity of tyranny, evil, injustices, and fatal persecution? Early Christians didn't die just to prove they were willing to die. They were accused of committing crimes against man-made laws and confronting injustices that directly opposed God's laws. They displayed relentless courage to make right the wrongs of their day and their actions made them a target. Religious and political leaders' authority and power were threatened by the very acts of a few brave souls. We will dive deeper into the cost of advancing Christianity in the next chapter.

Something new is being built, and there are only a few precious things we can take into this new era. A few of those things include a tenacious dedication to God's ways, a passion for prayer, relentless faithfulness to Jesus' church through deep, meaningful relationships. Each of these qualities were revered by the previous generations who pioneered the church in our nation. If we can embody these precious gifts from generations past, I believe we can move forward into the new, while being anchored in a solid foundation from the past.

Here are some questions to ask God about: Do I want to become more useful to Jesus during these opportune times? Do I have the courage to stand up in the areas God is asking of us? If your answer is yes, begin your new journey by seeking the Lord with an open heart, so you can receive a fresh perspective. A heavenly vantage point.

12

Undying Values

Several years ago, I was in Cuba on a missionary trip with my spiritual father. During my trip, we visited a Cuban pastor. I will call him Steven, to protect his name. You will see why a little later in the story.

Steven was in his late eighties, and he walked very slow. As he showed us around his small church, I could tell he was extremely proud of it. I noticed several young men who followed him around very closely and tended to his needs. I could tell Steven cared deeply for the young men, as if they were his own sons. I asked Steven if the young men were his children, and suddenly his demeanor changed as he explained that they are only his spiritual sons. My first thought was that he and his wife were unable to have children, but I didn't dare to ask. For some reason, he decided to share about his son. His story impacted the way I look at serving God's kingdom. In fact, I was never the same after he shared his story about his son.

Steven offered me a seat in his church a few rows away from his wife. As he got ready to tell me about his son, he glanced toward his wife who was a few rows away talking to the young men, and Steven lowered his voice so she wouldn't hear him. At that point, I knew he was about to tell me something important and heartbreaking.

Steven told me that they lost their only son after decades of trying to have children. He was close to fifty years old when they finally conceived their only child. I asked him if his son died during childbirth, but again, he glanced over at his wife and nodded his head side-to-side, quietly saying *no*. Steven told me His son was about twenty years old when he died.

In those days, the communist government was very harsh toward Christians. Any churches that taught the entire Bible were abolished and Christianity was outlawed. The pastors who dared to plant a new church met secretly in their homes. Breaking the law resulted in prison, death and their homes were taken after throwing the wives and children out on the streets. In fact, every person who proclaimed to be a Christian was blacklisted by the government, which meant they weren't permitted to work to make a living for their families. There was a big cost associated with becoming a Christian. Becoming a Christian cost people their livelihood, freedom and sometimes their lives.

Their government actively investigated rumors about secret churches. Pastors often went to jail and suffered extreme persecution. Steven was a pastor when the communist regime was at the peak of its power and controlled every move of its citizens.

One day Steven arrived home and the federal police were at his door with orders to take him away. He mentioned how often the government harassed him and threw him in jail on several occasions. The police were going to take him away, and his family was unsure whether they would ever see him again. As Steven was pleading with the police in his front yard, they pointed their guns at him. Steven's son dashed in front of his father to protect him, begging the police to leave him alone. As he stepped in front of his father one of the guns fired and hit the young man in the chest. Steven embraced his son as he slumped toward the ground with a fatal wound.

Steven wept as he told me this story. I saw deep pain in his watery eyes as he recounted the horrible day that his son, the pride and joy of his life, breathed his last breath. Steven's son died in his arms. His wife cried hysterically as the police handcuffed her husband, while her only son lay dead on the ground. Her son was murdered and her husband taken away, knowing she would never see either of them again.

Steven was thrown into the back of the police car while he watched his distraught wife holding his dead son in her arms, crying uncontrollably on her hands and knees. The police sped off without remorse or concern. Nobody called an ambulance or a mortuary.

As they drove away, they turned off the paved road onto a long dirt road in the middle of nowhere. He knew his fate was sealed. I asked Steven if he was scared, but all he could think about was losing his precious son and leaving his dear wife widowed. When the police found a desolate place to stop, they pulled over and yanked Steven out of the police car. After unholstering their guns, the police dispatcher called the police officers over the radio with an urgent situation. The police quickly jumped into their car and sped off, leaving Steven alone in the middle of nowhere.

God intervened and saved Steven from being murdered. He walked home and buried his son. Almost twenty years had passed by, at the time he told me the story. When Steven was finished telling me the story about his son, he took one last look at his wife to ensure she wasn't listening. Both parents were deeply hurt, even though nearly twenty years had gone by. Amazingly, Steven was more concerned with his wife's feelings of grief than he was about his own pain.

At that point, I had only heard and read stories of persecution, but I had never met anyone who endured such extreme forms of persecution. His story made me curious. Steven obviously never stopped being a pastor, nor did it stop his wife from serving Jesus. My mind was filled with questions. I asked Steven if he felt any regrets about being a pastor or serving Jesus. He looked at me with tears in his eyes and said, "I have no regrets. I wish my son was still alive, but it was not God's will. I will continue pastoring until the day the Lord takes me home". His words penetrated deep into my soul.

My spiritual father told me Steven had been a pastor to the entire city of pastors. A spiritual father to many sons and daughters, impacting the future of his city for God's kingdom.

I left Cuba a changed man. His story sent me on a new mission. When I arrived back home, I poured through the Bible to learn more about persecution. To my discovery, I learned that Jesus said we should expect it. The early church celebrated it, and the most impactful Christians honored it. Christians with this mindset about persecution become useful to God and he uses them to advance Christianity in the most significant ways. Their undying commitment to God's mission helped establish the church and changed the world forever.

I'm unsure whether Steven is still alive, but his story still resonates in my heart and drives me toward a higher standard of embracing persecution. After all these years, I am still on a mission to keep getting better at embracing persecution as an honor. Although I have never experienced the same levels of persecution, I desire to become more useful to God's mission. If He asks me to give away all my life's possessions or lay down my life for an impactful assignment, I only hope I will celebrate the privilege with honor. This man's story changed my life forever. It matured and strengthened me in ways I never knew possible. Every day since I met Steven, I focus on maturing me in areas of forgiveness, responding to persecution correctly and developing a willingness to let go of everything dear to me, all for God's mission. I ask Him daily to put me in situations that stretch me in these areas. My prayers have placed me in positions of uncertainty and constant change throughout my life. God has set me on an interesting path where every step seems unchartered and unknown to me. I've been afforded the privilege to partner with God concerning some things that grieve His heart.

Although I am unable to say that I would die for Jesus because I've never been tested to that degree, I hope to one day be self-assured that I could confidently say such a thing. Until then, I will keep seeking, praying and maturing.

Such acts of courage and love, like Steven's, undoubtedly impacted the church. I'm sure his church was encouraged and strengthened by the way both parents kept serving Jesus and building God's kingdom. From my perspective, the Lord showed me the tenacity He wants the church to possess. The church in Cuba exploded from about 2% of the population claimed to be Christians, to now around 25%. No wonder the church was so powerful. You can't kill that sort of love. As Satan raised the heat of intensity against the church, the stronger it became, the more God's kingdom spread.

The Lord is always ten steps ahead of Satan's diabolical plans. Jesus always turns bad situations into blessings. The worse the curse, the bigger the blessings. This story made me see Christianity in a different light. A burning question lingered in my mind all these years. How can the American church create the same cosmic gravity that will pull our world into God's divine family? Well, this chapter attempts to answer that question.

Before we answer the question, we will explore the early church's biblical values. Considering the story above, it's plain to see the gaps in the American church and our own lives. These gaps have created several weaknesses that have been exploited by Satan.

We lack critical values and principles that made the Cuban church such a divine force. Those values are similar to the first century church. We have become so focused on creating strategies to fill up seats, we neglect to instill certain biblical values the early church lived by—most importantly, the values they died for. They possessed an uncompromising mindset that led to martyrdom by execution, torture, beheading, burning, and all sorts of gruesome types of persecution. Early Christians refused to compromise and would rather put it all on the line.

Perhaps the most important part of their deaths was how they faced it, with an attitude of honor, feeling privileged to die for Jesus and His church. Although many martyrs died giving their lives away, their response was astonishing. Some showed joy, gratitude, and even forgiveness toward their murderers. Some of these brave Christians literally prayed for forgiveness for their persecutors while breathing their last breath. What an amazing display of kingdom perspective and an undying love for Jesus. No wonder the early church spread like wildfire. Every time Satan tried to stomp out their fire, the church spread under his foot of persecution.

God's love was reflected through their commitment and attitude, which allowed the Holy Spirit to penetrate the world's heart. Their valor encouraged and strengthened the early church during times of heavy persecution. I cannot imagine what it was like to establish the church in the world for the very first time. I'm sure it must have been extra difficult, especially since it was something mankind had never witnessed. It was a special achievement in history accomplished by very special people.

Today's church in America doesn't come close to being committed to Jesus or His cause on that level. Our voices have become quiet whispers in the background of the chaos. Somehow we have become too afraid, too soft, and too delicate. We need more tenacity and fortitude. Everything is geared toward a seeker-friendly mentality that caters to the comfort of church members. A small percentage of the people do all the work, while the majority of attendees drop a few dollars into the offering basket, acting as if they have earned a right to voice their heavy commands on running the church. It is a disgusting display of an anemic church too scared to offend anybody. Decades of drift have taken us to place where we are creating followers too ignorant about God's expectations to change our world. This trend needs to change so the church can get back into the fight.

The condition of our country requires a strong church that thrives under adversity. God can turn around our nation's church. Nothing is too hard for God. He has created a strong church in other countries, like Africa, China, Cuba, and South America. Jesus can certainty do it in America.

What can *we* do to fix it? Where do we start? Back to the basics. Leaders need to instill biblical values and Christ-centered qualities into the fabric of our church culture. These must be the overriding principles that govern everything we do, from the smallest part of our daily lives to the biggest visions for ministries that change the trajectory of our world. We need a higher level of expectation from every single believer. It's the only way America will achieve true freedom, which is God's ultimate goal for the gospel of Jesus Christ.

One thing is certain: kingdom building must never be dependent on buildings, budgets, or the talents of any single person. God's kingdom is about Jesus and His plans and purposes. Achieving them will take more than a team mentality. It will take a kingdom family, bound by His blood, willing to give everything for one another. The same way Jesus laid Himself down for us.

This is a depth of love that is only achievable through God's grace. When Jesus died for us, He redefined our shallow understanding of love. Jesus created a deeper love that dies for others. He said, "Greater love has no one than this: to lay down one's life for one's friends. You are my friends if you do what I command" (John 15:13-14).

Our goal is to achieve a Jesus level of love. Only then will we be capable of becoming the divine family Jesus intended. There's no doubt in my mind that God has been growing the maturity of His church over the past one hundred years. Gearing us up for this moment. The Holy Spirit is transforming us into a greater expression of His love and power. The face of God's church is radically changing. As the Holy Spirit draws a highly diverse people to

275

repentance, the Lord is grafting a new breed of believers into the church body. They cannot fit into the traditional molds and shortcomings of a church hard pressed to meet its own growing challenges. They seek a deeper love beyond our clever slogans and cute sermons. Those things are incapable of producing such depth of character, love, and sacrifice.

Although we have some gaps, the Holy Spirit is connecting the global church in unprecedented ways. We are seeing a new level of cooperation amongst the church body. Ministries and churches are connecting and uniting across the world. Ministers and leaders are partnering in impactful ways to reach and strengthen a new heavenly crop. The Holy Spirit is intertwining an international network of ministers and ministries. The global church is experiencing a broader and deeper level of unity with covenant relationships amongst like-minded kingdom builders committed to fulfilling Jesus' mandate to disciple the nations.

We finally are ready to review the Christian values Jesus requires from every Christian that loves Him. Before we dive into them, we must define the definition of values. Values are a set of principles we use as a standard to guide our everyday lives. We use guiding principles when faced with decisions in our everyday lives, including how we treat others, the way we respond to situations, how we raise our children, etc. Some of our values result in good things happening (blessings) and others put us in bad situations or create bad relationships around us.

Before I list this set of biblical values, it should be noted I did not come up with them on my own. I derived them from the Bible. The following values are not meant to be an exhaustive list; however, from a Biblical perspective, they seem to be the most critical. I have also chosen a scripture for each value that you will need to review for a fuller understanding.

First: Express your personal love for Jesus by the way you live, worshiping God with an obedient life.

"Anyone who loves me will obey my teaching. . . . Anyone who does not love me will not obey my teaching ." (John 14:23-24). This includes the way we lead God's church. More on that later.

Second: Consistent intimacy with Jesus.

277

"Now this is eternal life: that [we] know you, the only true God, and Jesus Christ, whom you have sent." (John 17:3). Everything good flows from our relationship with Jesus. An intimate and ever-growing relationship with Jesus is our life's foundation and will propel us into our destiny.

Third: Develop deep, meaningful relationships within our homes and amongst the church.

I've already written a lot about these things in previous chapters, plus you will see much more in the following chapters. So, I will list two brief verses that say it all in John 15:12-13: "My command is this: Love each other as I have loved you. . . . Lay down [your] life for [your] friends."

Fourth: Develop mature qualities of humility toward everyone, especially those who have hurt you.

"But the fruit of the Spirit is love, joy, peace, forbearance, kindness, goodness, faithfulness, gentleness and self-control." (Galatians 5:22-23).

Fifth: Embrace suffering and persecution joyfully, as an honor, because doing so brings glory to Jesus and strengthens His church.

The words of the apostle Paul hit home this point with eloquence and power, especially given that Paul had already proved his willingness to die for God's plans and purposes. In Philippians 3:10-16, Paul said,

> I want to know Christ – yes, to know the power of his resurrection and participation in his sufferings, becoming like him in his death, and so, somehow, attaining to the resurrection from the dead. Not that I have already obtained all this, or have already arrived at my goal, but I press on to take hold of that for which Christ Jesus took hold of me. Brothers and sisters, I do not consider myself yet to have taken hold of it. But one thing I do: forgetting what is behind and straining toward what is ahead, I press on toward the goal to win the prize for which God has called me heavenward in Christ Jesus. All of us, then, who are mature should take such a view of things. And if on some point you think differently, that too God will make clear to you. Only let us live up to what we have already attained.

Sixth: Make Spirit-filled disciple-makers who display the supernatural power of God to change our culture and align it with God's ways. "But you will receive power when the Holy Spirit comes on you; and you will be my witnesses in Jerusalem, and in all Judea and Samaria, and to the ends of the earth." (Acts 1:8).

Francis Chan created a similar list of values, which I learned in one of his trainings called, We Are Church. You can read more about his perspective in his book, Letters to the Church.

These values reflect the characteristics of the early church. Most importantly, they reflect the way Jesus lived and the reason He died. When we study the first century church, we will see how they embodied these values. They lived by these precious values, and more importantly, they died for them. Steven, the Cuban pastor, also lived by these values when his son was murdered because of his decision to change his city for Jesus. These values make God's church an unstoppable force under the most intense persecution. No doubt, instilling these values into our lives will propel our cities into a new future.

Spend time to uncover deeper biblical truths behind the list of values above. Personal study of Scripture will uncover deeper meaning than my meager vocabulary can express. The full expression of Jesus' church is far beyond my comprehension. Although I can only see a glimpse of her vast beauty, I do know one thing when it comes to kingdom building: God's ways are always better than our ways. His thinking is infinitely higher than ours, and our personal agendas or so-called innovative ideas are nothing more than shallow attempts to move forward in our own strength.

During the height of the Corona virus, the church was forced to create more meaningful relationships inside our homes and amongst our kingdom family. Many of us yearned for corporate gatherings, while countless others disconnected from the church altogether and drifted away from Jesus. We saw how easily people who consider themselves Christians can fall away from the church. The Lord taught us something about creating meaningful relationships in our homes and amongst the church. He forced the church to make a decision about deepening our faith. Unfortunately, some of the church decided to turn away from Jesus.

How can we embrace suffering and persecution if the church is unable to advance the kingdom when a pandemic keeps us home on Sundays? We need a major overhaul with respect to these important values.

Imagine for a moment that our churches actually loved one another to the point of death. What if we were willing to give up everything important to us for someone else's needs? We would display a depth of maturity the world is dying for. God's divine family would look like the only real solution to our fallen world. Our love for one another would create a cosmic gravity, pulling everyone into it.

Jesus was obviously conveying that depth of love in John 17:20-23 when He prayed for His new church.

> I pray also for those who will believe in me through their message, that all of them may be one, Father, just as you are in me and I am in you. May they also be in us so that the world may believe that you have sent me. I have given them the glory that you gave me that they may be one as we are one – I in them and you in me- so that they may be brought to complete unity. Then the world will know that you sent me and have loved them even as you have loved me.

When we begin to function with God's depth of love, our unity will reach a deeper level of maturity. Our united love will unlock the supernatural power of God and release it on earth. Then the love of Christ will speak into the hearts of every man, woman, and child. Just as the scripture above say, "Then the world will know that you sent me and have loved them even as you have loved me."

As you can see, unity means more than tolerating one another's theology or leveraging our kingdom network. Jesus created the church to be a body that needs one another to function according to God's commands. In other words, we need one another in much deeper ways than once imagined. Maturity is needed to become interdependent, relinquishing our selfish ideals of creating personal ministries with personal ambitions. Instead of creating our own clever plans and mission statements, we need to seek the Holy Spirit for His visions, and lock our arms to achieve God's strategies, being interconnected to fulfill God's plans and purposes. We need each other. You need me, and I need you, and together, we need the power of God to get the job done correctly. That's a different church than we have been building, which means everything needs to change.

Imagine an interdependent church where each believer finds their individual assignment and corresponding territory, seeking our prophets to confirm God's will for everywhere from our individual cities to our entire nation. Then we look to our apostles to create infrastructure and strategies, as we all find our places of responsibility within God's blueprints. Meanwhile, our evangelists begin executing the strategies by combing the streets, drawing people to Jesus, and stirring revival. We use the prophets and music ministers to decree God's plans and purposes throughout the land, while battling principalities. As the Holy Spirit swiftly spreads across the land, our pastors and teachers lead new converts into deep relationships within the church body and inside our homes, where believers are taught to follow God's ways in every aspect of their lives. Then the new believers become involved with their communities to change their culture, standing up for truth and righteousness in their workplaces, government, education systems, etc.

We would create renewed communities that produce biblical marriages with godly fathers and mothers, providing a new foundation producing blessed children who love the Lord and His ways. The new community will begin eradicating injustices and unrighteousness from every corner of their cities. Our unified efforts would begin eliminating homelessness, prostitution, rape, and dysfunctional homes.

I hope you get the picture. We would see a much more powerful church, an interdependent church, a single-minded church with no mavericks or superstars. Everyone would play an equal part. Dare I say we would function the same way as the early church did when the church in Antioch was established? No! I believe we need to learn from the past and do it better. Learning from the early church should only be our starting point. God's church must reach beyond the places it has already walked. The condition of our world demands it, and our love for one another is a bigger key than we realize. We need to unlock a deeper level of God's supernatural power through deeper sacrifices of love for one another.

Are we willing and able to go there? In my estimation, we are missing this key ingredient. It's love, and not just any love. It's a selfless Jesus love that puts God's plans and everyone else's needs in front of our own. It might sound cliché, but the longer I walk with Jesus the more apparent it becomes. It takes a Jesus-sized love to get it done. Love is the glue that binds all things: love within the church body; love for God's ways; love for God's purposes; love within our families; and a deep love that burns with pain and passion for the hurting and destitute. A love that pushes us into action to rectify our nation's condition.

We are simply not there yet, not as a church body and certainly not as a nation. What is the path to get there? Only in Scripture are such mysteries revealed. 2 Peter 1:3-8 describes a process of maturation, with steps that build upon each other.

His divine power has given us everything we need for a godly life through our knowledge of him who called us by his own glory and goodness. . . . you may participate in [Jesus'] divine nature, having escaped the corruption in the world caused by evil desires. For this very reason, make every effort to add to your faith goodness; and to goodness, knowledge; and to knowledge, self-control; and to self-control, perseverance; and to perseverance, godliness; and to godliness, mutual affection; and to mutual affection, love. For if you possess these qualities in increasing measure, they will keep you from being ineffective and unproductive in your knowledge of our Lord Jesus Christ.

Do you see how much it takes to achieve God's definition of love? It's difficult to attain such a high level of unconditional love. Verses 5 through 7 describe the path we need to build up our love. It's a lifelong process that seems to happen during phases in our lives, a small piece at a time. But the results are simply miraculous. I've created a graphic based upon the scriptures in 2 Peter 1. The graphic below depicts a roadmap leading to Jesus' example of agape love. I named it the Circle of Love.

Circle of Love

Notice how many elements it takes to grow our love. Seven different characteristics must grow to achieve it, and each one is interconnected. You could look at it as a cycle or a process. I like to think of it as a pathway that begins with faith and ends with love. Each step leads us into the next phase of our journey. Once we travel those phases of our path, our love is built up. A never-ending journey that builds upon itself and eventually creates a deeper love

287

within us. Each step creates a layer that acts as a foundation for the next layer.

Unfortunately, you will not find a fast track, nor are there any shortcuts. They do not exist. Your road will be hard, and it is supposed to be that way. We are a mess on the inside, and we always seem to embrace the Lord with one arm, while pushing Him away with the other. Most of the time, we are our own worst enemies. No wonder it takes the Lord so long to work within us—there are so many layers of issues to unravel. Although we get in His way, He is still able to somehow work. The Holy Spirit works with such loving care and patience, never giving up on us. His love is both relentless and tenacious. It never gives up, never gives in, and overcomes every obstacle we put in His way.

The path toward achieving God's standard of love is not just a cycle or a process, but a journey. It's a path that will prove to be the most difficult journey of your life because it requires you to travel deep within your darkest and most troublesome places. Become intentional building each attribute, asking the Holy Spirit to reveal and remove internal obstacles, and provide opportunities of growth through testing.

With the correct depth of love, we are capable of such great accomplishments for God's kingdom. Love will drive us forward when adversity tries to stop us. Following Jesus is not for the faint of heart. Only the brave will have the biggest kingdom impact. The Bible has some harsh things to say about those whose faith refuses to stand up for Jesus. In fact, Jesus Himself emphasizes it in Mark 8:28: "If anyone is ashamed of me and my words in this adulterous and sinful generation, the Son of Man will be ashamed of them when He comes in His Father's glory with the holy angels."

The Bible refers to such faithlessness as cowardly in Revelation 21:8, where it says, "But the cowardly, the unbeliever, the vile, the murderers, the sexually immoral, those who practice magic arts, the idolaters and all liars – they will be consigned to the fiery lake of burning sulfur. This is the second death."

This scripture puts cowards on the same level as unbelievers and murderers. As we can see, Scripture reveals a deeper truth about Jesus' expectations for His church. Our willingness to stand up for

God's ways goes much deeper and is more serious in His eyes than we realize.

The Bible has a lot more to say about persecution. Let's review a few scriptures to gain a well-rounded understand it.

Expect persecution: "In fact, everyone who wants to live a godly life in Christ Jesus will be persecuted" (2 Timothy 3:12).

Forms of persecution: "Blessed are you when men hate you, and ostracize you, and insult you, and scorn your name as evil, for the sake of the Son of Man" (Luke 6:22).

Do not fear persecution: "But even if you should suffer for the sake of righteousness, you are blessed. And do not fear their intimidation, and do not be troubled" (1 Peter 3:14).

Persecution is a blessing: "Blessed are those who are persecuted because of righteousness, for theirs is the kingdom of heaven. Blessed are you when people insult you, persecute you and falsely say all kinds of evil against you because of me. Rejoice and be glad, because great is your reward in heaven, for in the same way they persecuted the prophets who were before you" (Matthew 5:10-12).

Persecution brings glory: "If you are reviled for the name of Christ, you are blessed, because the Spirit of glory and of God rests on you" (1 Peter 4:14).

You can find many more scriptures about persecution. Study for yourself and you will see more clearly. Persecution is an honor and a blessing. When we get our minds right about persecution, fear will lose its grip on every believer. Embracing persecution as a privilege disarms Satan from using fear as a weapon. Responding correctly to persecution will strengthen the church to become bold and courageous. The correct mindset creates an air of expectation for the church to stand in the face of adversity, thereby creating a church that will stand for God's ways, plans, and purposes, facing hard times the way Jesus did while hanging on the cross and breathing His last breath for us.

More blessings flow from a correct response to persecution. A selfless response to persecution will preach without words. Our actions speak louder than words. Forgiveness displays the love of Christ and allows the Holy Spirit to work within those who want to harm us. A selfless response results in salvation from those who deny Jesus. It also matures the persecuted one and keeps sin from his or her heart. As you can see, it's not about us. It's about obedience in the face of adversity. Our future is sealed with God, and our eternity lies where Jesus resides. Our lives here on earth have a purpose. If our lives (or our deaths) bring others to the cross, we have fulfilled our eternal purpose.

When Jesus said, "If anyone would come after me, let him deny himself and take up his cross and follow me. For whoever would save his life will lose it, but whoever loses his life for my sake will find it" (Matthew 16:24).

Jesus literally meant we must give Him our lives. When we accept Jesus as our Savior, we make a life-commitment that extends into eternity. His command to us is to lay down our life to advance His kingdom, stand for truth, and live a selfless life for His cause. This life is no longer about us, our needs, or our dreams. Our new life is about God's dreams and His plans. Our responsibility is to figure out our part in His future.

Isaiah 7:9 says, "If you do not stand firm in your faith, you will not stand at all."

I read an article that sums it up well: "Yes, there is a cause. Christianity is not a vacation, not a cruise, but a cause. Issues that affect the destiny of human beings must not be ignored. Crucial truths cannot be sacrificed on the altar of toleration or diplomacy. We cannot cry, peace, peace, when there is no peace! It is sinful for the people of God to shrink back in fear in the face of the enemy. The Lord has not given His church a spirit of fearfulness."[i]

The church needs to move past its spiritual rhetoric and get its hands on the plow of instilling integrity into every facet of our culture. Quit blaming everything on spiritual warfare. Our nation's moral decline is a cancer and it's killing our families. If we refocus our efforts on biblical values, spiritual forces will be rendered powerless.

By no means am I saying Satan's army will stop trying to destroy us. I'm simply saying we are overly focused on the demonic. It has become our excuse, as if we are victimized. In reality, we are a product of our own decisions. For example, we can't blame Satan for our failed marriages or our recurring sin. It's our selfish ways and a desire to have things our way.

293

Hopefully by now, you are seeing the simple truth and the importance of Christian values. If we consider ourselves a follower of Jesus, then it is our responsibility to instill these values into our sphere of influence. Instill them by following the values yourself, prioritizing them in your areas of ministry, and teaching them to your children.

Too many sermons are preached from pulpits across the nation with a shallow version of God's truths. Consequently, Christians believe they should have a trouble-free life after accepting Jesus as Lord of their heart. The truth is happiness and prosperity are temporary comforts unrelated to following Jesus. Jesus never promised a trouble-free life. Nor does He promise prosperity and an easy life. He only promised to lighten our burdens when we experience difficult circumstances. In fact, Jesus spoke clearly about the hard times we will experience because of our choice to follow Him.

Persecution is expected. An attitude of gratitude will make us more useful to God because the correct response makes all the difference.

A great example is in Acts 5:41-42, which says, "The apostles left the Sanhedrin, rejoicing because they had been counted worthy of suffering disgrace for the Name [of Jesus]. Day after day . . . they never stopped teaching and proclaiming the good news that Jesus is the Messiah."

The apostles' brave response to persecution strengthened and encouraged the church. Their actions spoke without words and set a standard for everyone else to follow. God used persecution to strengthen the church. God is so masterful at turning the tables on Satan's diabolical plans. Just look at our very lives. Look at where Jesus brought us from. Jesus made something good from our lives, and that's all the proof we need to convince us. He is the Master at turning bad situations into a good outcome.

The church suffered persecution in ways never expected. Acts 8:1-8 says, "On that day a great persecution broke out against the church in Jerusalem, and all except the apostles were scattered. . . . But Saul [Paul] began to destroy the church. . . . He dragged off both men and women and put them in prison. . . . Those who had been scattered preached the word wherever they went. . . . So there was great joy in that city."

The church responded correctly to persecution, and again their correct response allowed them to keep focused. They continued spreading the good news about Jesus Christ. Although Satan tried scattering the church, God turned the tables and used Satan's plans to spread the church and advance Christianity. Jesus worked mightily through the church's willingness to embrace persecution. Every time the world tried to stomp out the fire of the church, it spread like a spark that grew into a forest fire.

What happens when we respond incorrectly, when we are too immature or overly focused on our own bad situations?

Mark 4:17 says, "But since they have no root, they last only a short time. When trouble or persecution comes because of the word, they quickly fall away."

You can fall away or become useless to the kingdom when you repeatedly respond the wrong way.

What should you do the next time you experience persecution?

Bless them: Romans 12:14 says, "Bless those who persecute you, bless and do not curse."

Love and pray for them: Matthew 5:44 says, "But I tell you, love your enemies and pray for those who persecute you."

These responses will keep you from becoming bitter, angry, oppressed, etc. Your correct response guards you from demons trying to control you with pain, past hurts, rejection, etc. Selfless love frustrates the enemy's plans to overtake you.

There is one more thing that isn't talked about very much. People who hurt you will face Jesus one day. It is well known that God's will for every person is to accept Jesus and spend eternity with Him. The last thing on our minds should be revenge or God's judgment. On the contrary, we should pray for God's mercy and patience for those who mistreat us or cause suffering in our lives. God's hand of judgment is eternal, and we should never wish eternal judgement upon anyone. Those types of prayers are considered witchcraft.

Let's take it to the next level of maturity. If you are the type of Christian asking God to grow and stretch you toward new levels of maturity and usefulness, this next scripture is for you. In fact, it will probably be something you will work on for the rest of your life. James 1:2-4 says, "Consider it pure joy, my brothers and sisters, whenever you face trials of many kinds, because you know that the testing of your faith produces perseverance. Let the perseverance finish its work so that you may be mature and complete, not lacking anything."

This is a hard scripture to achieve. We need lots of God's grace and the right attitude. It can make a big difference if we work on it daily. We can see what it did for Paul in this profound statement he made in 2 Corinthians 12:10: "That is why, for Christ's sake, I delight in weaknesses, in insults, in hardships, in persecutions, in difficulties. For when I am weak, then I am strong."

Paul endured extreme levels of suffering and persecution for the gospel. His relentless dedication to God's plans and purposes matured him to a rare and honorable place. Read Paul's words in Acts 21:13. "I am ready not only to be bound, but also to die in Jerusalem for the name of the Lord Jesus."

Paul embraced death and he refused to let its threat dissuade him from God's mission. Revelation 2:10 says, "Do not be afraid of what you are about to suffer. I tell you, the devil will put some of you in prison to test you, and you will suffer persecution for ten days. Be faithful, even to the point of death, and I will give you life as your victor's crown."

Persecution is a sign that Jesus will be back soon. Look what Jesus said about it in Matthew 24:7-10. "Nation will rise against nation, and kingdom against kingdom. There will be famines and earthquakes in various places. All these are the beginning of birth pains. *Then* you will be handed over to be persecuted and put to death, *and* you will be hated by all nations because of me. At that time *many* will turn away from the faith and will betray and hate each other" (emphasis added).

I am not trying to paint a grim picture about following Jesus or advancing Christianity. Just the opposite. My goal is to recalibrate our mindsets for the mission, removing the obstacle of fear from our life's destiny.

God has a greater plan in store for us and His church, and we must not allow anything to stand in the way. How will the church's leadership respond to God's commands to build His church the way

He wants it? Take time to pray daily. Seek God's voice of direction. Partner with some prophets and apostles in seeking God for answers. And most of all, have courage to obey the path He gives.

Radical times require a high level of obedience. Unfortunately, many Christians think persecution is a sacrifice. For the most part, the American church does not experience any extreme forms of persecution. Our freedoms of religion have afforded us a form of comfortable Christianity. On top of that, most Americans act as if we are special, and we deserve all the best things life has to offer. When you combine a mindset of comfortable Christianity with our sense of entitlement, it creates a toxic mixture. The church in our nation needs to allow God's Word to renew our mindsets about persecution. Our expectation for persecution needs a paradigm shift. We need to toughen up, show more grit, and count it a privilege to stand for truth, justice, and righteousness. I believe it is one of the single most important values that will allow the Holy Spirit to launch us into a new level of effectiveness.

We can start by taking a stand with love, mercy, and grace. We must be the light and stand for truth, righteousness, and justice in the face of adversity. But it's not our place to condemn God's church or the world around us with judgmental criticism. Jesus didn't condemn the world, but He became condemned on our behalf. We can still stand up for truth without condemning people living in the dark, by staying focused on God's righteousness without being judgmental, and standing on the side of justice without speaking curses on others.

Simply put, we are supposed to be the "light and salt" on earth. It means we stand against corruption, while we show grace toward the offenders. We are supposed to give our lives for truth, while we represent Jesus' everlasting love and walk in God's ways while facing persecution. We are to smile at our accusers, knowing we are ambassadors for the risen King. The same way Jesus loves us. It will encourage the church, shine light on evil, and draw the lost to the cross.

John F. Kennedy made a powerful statement in his presidential inaugural address. He said, "We shall pay any price, bear any burden, meet any hardship, support any friend, oppose any foe to assure the survival and success of liberty."

Our culture almost seems to parallel the conditions in Nehemiah 13, where their culture was wicked, and the church wandered from its rightful place. Nonetheless, Nehemiah assumed the responsibility to realign Jerusalem's culture with God's ways. Each step appeared insurmountable with obstacles at every turn. Nehemiah's assignment was made possible by God's hand, His direction, and a united effort from each person who loved God.

As a church body, our task at hand is to do the same thing. I'll call it kingdom realignment. To accomplish this, we need to create leaders who will change the world's ways. I pray that God convict every Christian, pastor, and ministry leader.

As we instill those critical values and they become part of our everyday lives, it will create an unwavering fortitude within us, a driving force necessary to achieve our ultimate calling—the call to fulfill the Great Commission.

As believers, we need to assume our place of authority for the world's systems, institutions, and culture. We are responsible for those things because God created this planet for us, not for Satan to rule.

Once the collective church begins shouldering its God-given assignment, our responsibilities will turn into our mission. We will begin viewing earth from a heavenly vantage point, where the entire world and its ways are our new pulpit. Then, and possibly only then, will America's destiny be realized—a destiny that God has appointed and anointed for our great nation to be a light unto the world.

How will God's church respond?

13

You Are Destined

We have been building up to an important topic, and it's time we get right to the heart of the matter. I'm talking about destiny: your destiny, the reason you were born and the purpose for your life.

This moment in time has the potential to be the greatest God-ordained moment our nation has ever seen. God created the church for moments like these to shine its brightest. We, as God's church, need to start *being* the church and stop merely *attending* a church. God has destined us for so much more than that.

Our collective destinies are tied to this moment. If your soul is deeply stirred about the things you have read thus far, I believe you have been God-ordained for His most significant purposes. Every person who is willing to follow Jesus can become a leader in God's kingdom, regardless of our past life, self-worth, or lack of abilities. God's grace will make a way for our destiny.

We need believers who are willing to accept the call to an unwavering commitment to lead the way. For those who are willing, leadership is within reach for every believer. Contrary to popular belief, the most effective leaders are not born with natural abilities. They are forged in the furnace of adversity. Leadership is comprised of specific qualities that are learned over time with focused diligence. Becoming a great leader develops as we master the art of living a disciplined life. Discipline and persistence are the *secret sauce* to becoming a leader in God's eyes. Impactful leaders possess specific biblical characteristics that must be developed over time.

In this chapter, you will find out how to reach your highest levels of kingdom impact through leadership. To be clear, leadership requires us to first build a foundation of the critical fundamentals from the previous chapters. Think of leadership characteristics like a building and think of Christian values as your foundation. The depth of our foundation determines what type of structure that can be built on it. For example, a skyscraper cannot be built on top of a foundation that is built for a house. The depth of our foundation dictates the heights that our leadership will rise. With a strong foundation, the sky is the limit.

Have you ever wondered what separates good leaders from great leaders? It's probably different than what you think. Many people think we need charisma, popularity, supreme intelligence, or some mysterious "*it*" factor that seems beyond your reach. None of those things makes a great leader. Anointing and calling have a lot to do with our influence in God's kingdom, but character takes us to levels of effectiveness where talent alone is incapable.

In our culture, leaders are usually associated with success. However, we will not use the word success because it is subjective and usually focuses on the wrong outcomes. Success is usually based on title, wealth, popularity, or other shallow and self-fulfilling attributes. Instead, we will focus on becoming an effective leader. Effectiveness is a much more tangible goal and a better way to think about leadership. Plus, effective leaders are more useful instruments to God compared to leaders who are searching for success. Each of us can become an effective leader because leadership characteristics can be developed over time. However, before you start improving your leadership qualities, keep in mind they are built upon a foundation of the Christian values we have already talked about exhaustively. Becoming disciplined in faithfulness and ever-growing obedience ensures our talent never takes us beyond our character's foundation.

Here are four critical leadership characteristics that will make you a highly effective leader. Each characteristic is based on biblical principles, which means we will become an effective leader in every facet of our life. Master them, and they will help you excel as a leader in business, government, church, your marriage, and leading the charge to change our nation.

First: Develop a mindset of servanthood. Leading means you want to help others find and fulfill their God-given destinies. Jesus said in Matthew 20:26-28, "Whoever wants to become great among you must be your servant, and whoever wants to be first must be your slave – just as the Son of Man did not come to be served, but to serve, and to give his life as a ransom for many." Never lead God's kingdom if your desires are to become great, famous, or the center of attention. God's kingdom is about advancing His agenda and developing the people around you.

Second: Remain teachable and embrace correction. Search God's Word for new truths about the way you lead and implement new truths as you go. Proverbs 1:2-5, 7 say, "For gaining wisdom and instruction; for understanding words of insight; for receiving instruction in prudent behavior, doing what is right and just and fair; for giving prudence to those who are simple, knowledge and discretion to the young – let the wise listen and add to their learning, and let the discerning get guidance." "The fear of the Lord is the beginning of knowledge, but fools despise wisdom and instruction." When the Holy Spirit reveals errors in our ways, the way we lead or live, our theology, or any area of our life, we accept our mistakes and take ownership without blaming others. Viewing our mistakes as opportunities to improve gives us the right attitude toward continuous improvement. A teachable mindset will drive us to keep learning and getting better when it comes to aligning with God's ways over our lifetime.

Third: Establish a lifestyle of consistent biblical character that has been tested during adversity. The scripture in 1 Timothy 3 defines the qualifications to become a leader in God's kingdom. Use those qualifications for yourself and those you lead. Although they are critical for each of us, we will focus the portion of scripture in 1 Timothy 3:10 that discusses being tested. "They [leaders] must first be tested; and then if there is nothing against them, let them serve." This scripture is telling us that our character must be tested before we enter leadership. Our character should remain consistent during all situations we encounter, whether our life is going well or everything is going extremely wrong. In my experience, there are three specific situations we should be tested. How we respond during these specific situations usually reveals deeper character flaws that are most destructive. How do we respond when: 1) We make catastrophic mistakes; 2) We experience extreme duress; 3) Important circumstances do not go the way we desire? Our response to these situations reveals our character and can provide opportunities for teachable leaders to improve.

309

Fourth: Lead as a unified team. Every person possesses an important role, and we need every person to find themselves and find their place in God's kingdom so each person can contribute. Function as a team, relying on each person's unique gifts and talents to grow God's kingdom. Let's read 1 Corinthians 12:7-11 & 22-27.

> Now to each one the manifestation of the Spirit is given for the common good. To one there is given through the Spirit a message of wisdom, to another a message of knowledge by means of the same Spirit, to another faith by the same Spirit, to another gifts of healing by that one Spirit, to another miraculous powers, to another prophecy, to another distinguishing between spirits, to another speaking in different kinds of tongues, and to still another the interpretation of tongues. All these are the work of one and the same Spirit, and he distributes them to each one, just as he determines.

> Those parts of the body that seem to be weaker are indispensable, and the parts that we think are less honorable we treat with special honor. And the parts that are unpresentable are treated with special modesty, while our presentable parts need no special treatment. But God has put the body together, giving greater honor to the parts that lacked it, so that there should be no division in the body, but that its parts should have equal concern for each other. If one part suffers, every part suffers with it; if one part is honored, every part rejoices with it. Now you are the body of Christ, and each one of you is a part of it.

We are the body of Jesus Christ, and we belong to Him. God's plans of redemption were established when He spoke the world into existence, which means He established the laws we must abide by. Jesus commanded us to function in harmonious unity. Truthfully, we are unable to grasp a full understanding of what unity is supposed to look like, nor do we know how to function with such interdependence. The Holy Spirit is taking His church to deeper unity; one step at a time and one generation at a time.

If you are already a leader and have mastered the leadership characteristics above, your job is to intentionally instill them into the men and women you are mentoring. Create disciples who reflect these characteristics and become masterful at instilling them into disciple-makers. It will help make us a masterful kingdom builder. "By the grace God has given me, I laid a foundation as a wise builder, and someone else is building on it. But each one should build with care." (1 Corinthians 3:10).

Advancing God's kingdom in truth, righteousness and justice is the most difficult thing we will ever do. At the same time, it is the most *rewarding* thing we will ever do. Always keep in mind, Jesus holds the blueprints to His kingdom plans, and I believe they are buried in His Word and within an intimate relationship with Jesus.

Our responsibility is to study, seek revelation from the Lord and keep ourselves aligned with His plans. Sounds simple but it is much more difficult than it sounds.

311

We can discover God's plans during our intimate time with the Lord. In fact, we will discover ourselves as our relationship with Jesus deepens over our lifetime. He will reveal more significant plans and purposes for our lives, which unveils our identity.

To summarize the things we need to advance God's kingdom, there are three essential ingredients: The Word of God, the Spirit of God, and the people of God. Never lose sight of this truth. All of God's greatest plans flow from these things. So, hold on to your methods loosely. Never prioritize methods or systems over truth. The first century church didn't have a systematic approach, only integrity and biblical values. Building God's kingdom should never overemphasize systems. The types of disciples we create is more important than having a well-oiled machine with great systems in place. Systems are useful to a degree. Mostly, they are nothing more than man-made attempts to apply business methods on God's kingdom. God's kingdom is not a business. It is a divine family.

Relying on systems too heavily, or applying them too much, usually results in creating limitations on God when attempting to develop disciples with deep substance and character. Most of the outcomes from a perfect system result in shallow followers who lack high obedience or deep relationship with Jesus. I'll end this subject by simply saying that Jesus commanded us to build a family who possess a rich relationship with Him and each other, while exhibiting high obedience and high multiplication.

Before I end this chapter, I'd like to give you a few keys to success, longevity, and a lifetime of growth. I've given you several lists of values and characteristics. But these keys are different. I want to pass along a few things that I value because they have allowed me to be extremely influential and effective in every area of my life. They will prove to be invaluable in every Christian's life:

- Stay transparent and honest in all your relationships. It's the fastest path to earning trust, and you will become highly influential in people's lives.

- Stay watchful for divine relationships. Make time for the people God puts in your path. Build those relationships with intentionality. Seek God's will and take courage to follow these relationships wherever He takes it.

- Get comfortable with being stretched and never let fear or insecurities rule you.

- Work hard to make the most of every God-opportunity, especially when you don't know where it will take you.

- Keep a mindset of dependency on Jesus. Protect your faith because it is much shallower than you realize.

- Accept yourself for who you are today. Be comfortable in your own skin. Embracing who you are, at this moment in your life, is the best path toward finding your best self.

- Set aside your own dreams, plans, and purposes. Seek God's dreams. Dare to dream with God.

- Stay true to yourself, even if it costs you your job, position of authority, or social status. Resist compromising your values and ethics because they are the building blocks that define your identity. An identity is hard to find and easier to lose than you think, especially when your character is put to the test. Losing your character through small compromises usually happens over time. It's a journey of small incremental missteps, and it's much harder to find your way back once you relinquish your values.

Values and ethics are tangible leadership characteristics anyone can achieve. You can become great in God's kingdom if you can master the art of discipline, faithfulness, and obedience in the ways you lead. Now that you know the *secret sauce* to becoming an impactful leader, you can start traveling toward your biggest destiny.

We are going to shift gears to talk about one of the most important topics for this new generation. This new generation of Christians needs strong and selfless spiritual fathers and mothers. The family unit in our nation does not look the same as God intended. The relationships within marriages and families have been totally distorted and destroyed by the enemy. They are broken beyond all recognition. It is the reason our nation is struggling so hard to fulfill the Dominion Mandate!

There is an epidemic in our country when it comes to absent fathers. There is a worse problem inside the church when it comes to the lack of spiritual fathers. The church today is in desperate need of spiritual fathers and mothers who can lead with integrity, character, and transparency. We need godly leaders who know how to love the unlovable with great patience and deep care. We've had our fill from the leaders who are self-centered, insecure, and unwilling to be taught. They have done a ton of damage and we deal with the effects every day. These leaders give us all a bad name and we are always trying to undo their damage. They wound people deeply and they get people all twisted up with harsh leadership and legalistic trash. They obscure God's grace by creating a false mindset of earning our way to heaven. These things must change because the new breed of leaders need strong, loving spiritual parents. Here's some insight that will help us understand why spiritual parenting is so critical for this new generation of followers.

God is raising up a new breed of leaders who come from dysfunctional lives. They have been betrayed, abandoned, abused, and cut deep by their own fathers, mothers, and family members. The fathers that abandoned their families have inflicted deep wounds that may never heal completely. There are a few fathers that stuck around, but they only wreaked havoc on their children and wives. Many fathers caused worse damage by sticking around than if they had left. There would have been far less trauma inflicted if they had abandoned their families.

These dysfunctional families have destroyed entire generations of children. They have created vicious cycles, getting worse with each generation. The cycles have produced adults trying to sort through the rubble in their lives, leaving them lost, trying to put together all the shattered pieces. They make hopeless efforts to fill giant voids of emptiness and pain, leading them to a never-ending appetite for extreme violence, heavy addictions, and twisted mentalities. They end up inflicting pain on others to get revenge from their past. They seem bent on destroying everything and everyone around them and the cycle spirals out of control, getting worse with each generation. Some turn to gangs as children and sell drugs before they are old enough to drive a car.

This massive damage has distorted their view of the world and God's love. They never had a good example to follow and now find themselves learning from scratch with their own children, not knowing know how to be fathers, husbands, wives, mothers, or daughters. What they need most are spiritual parents who will love

317

them with great care and patience with a love that lasts a lifetime, through thick and thin and the ugly. Spiritual parents are needed to provide guidance, with loving care, to set the proper example. With the proper spiritual parents, we can produce strong leaders who are healthy and whole.

God's church must take the lead to change our culture. Leading during these times requires a new dependence on Jesus—again. We cannot fall back on our past experiences, methods, and models. Old tricks won't get new results. This battle is far too big for that. It takes humility of heart because we must strip away every piece of ourselves that wants to rely on our own power to do this.

Start afresh by seeking God's will to understand higher visions and develop deeper strategies. Start asking God what He wants. What is He doing? How can we play our part? We need another level of faith, a bigger portion of favor, and a mindset renewed by the Word and the voice of God. Dare to dream with God and begin realigning our culture and our nation. We need a stronger church filled with power, love, and faith.

Start seeking God and ask Him how you can best serve His plans.

14

Defending America's Destiny

America is a highly blessed nation. It is often referred to as the land of opportunity, where we can create our own future. Most Americans fail to realize the extent of the average person's wealth in our country, especially if we have never visited third world countries. We possess an extreme level of wealth compared to most countries throughout the world. Most of the world is not afforded the same luxuries or opportunities that we have.

On top of our wealth, we possess the most powerful military the world has ever seen. There is no doubt God's hand of blessing is behind these things. God has been faithful to our country in many ways. But have you ever wondered why God chose to bless our nation so much more than almost every other country in history? There is a reason behind it all because we do not deserve God's blessings just for being born in the U.S. His faithfulness in blessing America goes way back to the time when our country was founded.

Our nation was established by our forefathers with biblical principles woven into every part of their culture. A love for Jesus and following His ways were the driving force behind establishing our great nation. God's ways were an integral part of the early settlers' everyday lives. You can plainly see evidence of it by reading a couple critical founding documents, such as the Declaration of Independence and the U.S. Constitution. Go read those documents for yourself. You will see a love for God and His Word embedded in the mindsets of our forefathers' belief systems. Their ideals and goals were to create a society that loves Jesus and walks in His ways.

Unfortunately, our country has strayed far from those ideals. While it is true that God will bless those who live according to His ways, our society does not value godliness today. So why is our nation still blessed? Should we live in a cursed land according to the Bible because of our nation's sin? There must be another reason God is still blessing us after all this time, especially given the fact our nation has become so wicked and corrupt.

There is only one reason God holds back curses from a nation that rebels against Him and His ways. You can find the reason when you look at Israel. God showed an endless amount of mercy when Israel rebelled against Him. They did not get what they deserved, at least not right away. God tried over and over to help Israel keep the covenant between God and Abraham, but Israel refused to keep their end of the deal. In fact, the entire Old Testament records the history of God's faithfulness to fulfill His covenant with Israel's forefathers.

When reading about Israel, it is obvious that our nation's forefathers made a promise with God. A covenant between God and the earliest of settlers, the very settlers who first came to this land with the intention of establishing a nation whose builder was God and whose foundation was His Word. Our nation was supposed to be a Christ-centered society, free to love Jesus and follow His ways, a dreamland where a new future was possible for generations to come. Their intention was to create a land that could shine the light of Jesus and be a beacon of hope for the world to see what happens when we establish a nation on God and His ways. The founding fathers put their own lives at stake to establish a nation where generational blessings would endure forever.

You can find proof of our forefathers' covenant with God in numerous monuments and founding documents created by our nation's forefathers. I'm going to tell you about one such national monument in Plymouth, Massachusetts. It's called The National Monument to the Forefathers. It is an awe-inspiring monument. There is something very special about it, almost holy and sacred. I'm going to briefly describe different aspects of the monument to highlight some of the critical attributes and their significance. Take a moment to look at the monument in Wikipedia by searching the National Monument to the Forefathers. Read the history about why it was built and the meaning behind each component of the statue. You can also study our nation's roots to better understand the statements I make in this chapter about our forefathers' covenant with God.

While you are reading my description of the monument, refer to the picture from the internet. The monument stands eighty-one feet tall and took nearly thirty years to build. It's made from a solid piece of granite and incorporates five different statues and numerous engravings. Each element of the statue has its own individual meaning, while collectively symbolizing an interwoven biblical culture our forefathers promised to build our country. As I try my best to describe the monument, imagine how the symbolism represents a promise to God about creating a society with God's ways at the center of it all. In fact, find an image of it on the internet while I describe its elements. Try to imagine that our forefathers are sending us a message through this monument. They are handing us a blueprint of the culture they promised God to build. It's the biblical blueprint we must use to realign our culture.

Standing atop an enormous foundation and platform is a woman named Faith, pointing toward heaven with her right hand and holding an old, tattered Bible in her left. Surrounding Faith's large foundation are four statues sitting in chairs facing outward. Each statue has its own name: Morality, Law, Education, and Liberty.

Collectively, the four statues represent the basic elements of the culture our forefathers promised God they would create. Each of the four statues surrounding Faith have additional engravings underneath them. The engravings represent biblical principles upon which each cultural element rests.

The first statue is Morality, which sits upon a Prophet and an Evangelist.

The second is Law, which sits upon Justice and Mercy.

The third is Education, with Youth and Wisdom underneath.

Finally, the fourth statue is a warrior named Liberty, and he sits above Tyranny Overthrown and Peace. Liberty holds a sword in his right hand and his left hand holds broken shackles. Every facet of the monument is steeped in biblical symbolism. You must see it for yourself to soak it all in.

Positioned between the four seated statues are four panels. Each panel contains engraved words to memorialize the ideals of the first settlers and their future nation.

The statements on two of the panels were particularly interesting and immediately grabbed my attention. These powerful words show the kingdom mindset of our founding fathers' undying determination to build a nation that follows God's ways. The front panel says, "National Monument to the Forefathers. Erected by a grateful people

325

in remembrance of their labors, sacrifices, and sufferings for the cause of civil and religious liberty." This statement represents the pilgrims' sacrifice to advance God's kingdom for their future generations in America.

On the rear panel is an engraved quote from William Bradford, who was the Governor of Plymouth, Massachusetts, during the first generation of pilgrims. As you read this powerful quote, try to imagine this small colony of first-generation Americans, all alone on an enormous and unsettled continent with nothing more than a dream and a promise to God. They were a determined people, risking life and family in pursuit of a God-appointed destiny. The inscription reads, "Thus out of small beginnings greater things have been produced by His hand that made all things of nothing and gives being to all things that are; and as one small candle may light a thousand, so the light here kindled hath shone unto many, yea in some sort to our whole nation; let the glorious name of Jehovah have all praise."

William Bradford's quote was a prophetic declaration for America to become a beacon of light, shining bright for Jesus. His sacred words represent the ultimate form of advancing Christianity globally, from which was established the most blessed nation on the planet, forever memorializing a prophetic vision for the destiny of our great nation. They were seeds of destiny, which were planted within a covenant and born through sacrifice and suffering.

Can it be that our willingness to endure persecution for the advancement of God's kingdom will help us turn our nation around? Can the actions of our faith activate our nation's greatest destiny? Can it be that our country's greatest years still lie ahead of us? Only God knows. But one thing is for sure: God always keeps His end of a covenant. The rest is up to us.

The National Monument to the Forefathers is our blueprint to create a blessed society. It represents our forefathers' original plans and cultural goals. Now the church can use it as our mission, by which we can create strategies to realign our country. Simply stated, it's our guide to fulfill the covenant that our forefathers made with God.

As we evaluate this roadmap, compare our society's current ways with each of the five elements on the monument. Determine for yourself how far we have drifted.

At this point in the book, we have come full circle with Chapter 9, where I provided an example of how Satan has turned our own systems and institutions against us. Take a moment and reread the section in Chapter 9 where I used the graphic of a chess board to depict our current state. Notice how the king is missing from the board.

In that section, I stated that Satan has removed the real King from the fabric of our culture. I hope you are beginning to see more clearly how Satan has been systematically removing God's ways from every facet of our values. Of course, it didn't happen all at once. Rather, there was a series of very small steps removing us from our covenant with God. As we drifted further and further away, our mission changed, our ideals changed, and eventually our god changed.

The previous chapters have taken us on a journey through every area of our culture, and we have explored many things that are wrong. We have also touched on some things we can do now to start making a difference. Hopefully, the Holy Spirit has already begun stirring your soul and leading you toward your next steps. However, this is only the beginning. Reforming our culture is a God-sized job and it will take all of us. We need a deeper form of unity to get it done. I need you, you need me, and we need each other. Now that we have a blueprint, we can all shoot for the same goal. A united church with locked arms, fighting for our destiny. As we begin moving toward implementing our nation's cultural foundations, liberty will be established. A new freedom will rule the land, whose foundation is God's truth.

If we don't change our culture, what will happen in the future? What will become of our great nation? Only God knows. One thing is for sure. God will be glorified, one way or the other. Our nation was born to glorify God's hand of grace. There are two clear paths for our future. Either we will follow His ways and our great nation will continue prospering from God's storehouse, or our society will continue removing God's ways and the name of Jesus from every facet of our culture. If the latter happens, things could go from bad to worse. God forbid it gets worse; however, if it does, God will use our sin to show the world His grace. One way or another, our nation's destiny will be fulfilled. Hopefully, it isn't the hard way.

I wholeheartedly believe our nation's destiny will be achieved. God's promises never fall to the ground. God's plans and purposes always come through, even when we fail to keep our end of the deal. If our selfishness and sin cause us to drift away on the easy road, we could end up learning the hard way. All the while, God will be glorified for the wickedness He delivers us from, the patience He shows through our journey, and the great care He takes doing it all.

Take Israel as an example. God promised to bless the world through them with a king. Although Israel did not keep their end of the deal, God did. Jesus still came to the earth to offer salvation for humanity. Israel suffered for their relentless sin, but Jesus was glorified, and Israel's destiny was ultimately fulfilled. Israel's destiny did not play out the way they had imagined. Nonetheless, a beacon of light was born.

Having said all of this, I only pray we can do it differently. Taking the blessed road instead of the road that involves God's judgment. Either way, God's kingdom will flourish, and America's destiny will prevail.

Will it all end in the collapse of our nation as we know it today? It's possible. But the fact is, God has a way of turning our broken covenants into blessings. He pulls blessings out of our sin. He finds a way to turn the tables on Satan's diabolical plans. Only time will tell.

Meanwhile, we have a job to do. Our job is not over until the job is done.

Ask the Lord, what can I do next? Begin by praying. Pray for revelation. Pray for wisdom. Pray for understanding. Pray for favor. Pray like you mean it. Pray until you hear something. Pray like Jesus did in the garden. Pray like Ezra and Nehemiah did when they heard about the condition of their people and their land through painful weeping that only came from deep concern for the condition of their people. Painful prayers poured out like tears of blood, and a move of God was born. Vision was imparted, favor was granted, and God moved in the greatest ways ever witnessed by mankind. The world witnessed the undeniable glory of God.

15

A New Dawn

A spiritual war is being fought on American soil and Satan is leading the charge. Extreme chaos has risen from the craziness of COVID. Human trafficking crimes are on the rise. Racially fueled conflicts are intensifying across our country. Fear is feeding conflict, while rioting and looting promote lawlessness. Our society has embraced abortion and same sex marriage, destroying our families and redefining God' sacred institution of marriage. Our youth and young adults are confused about their identities, causing the suicide rates to increase. Meanwhile, media is compounding the confusion and clouding politically motivated schemes for power.

At face value things look hopeless. Whether or not you can see it, God is on the move behind the scenes, turning Satan's diabolical plans against him. In fact, there is much more to God's plan than that. While Satan thinks he is turning our country into an anti-Christ nation, I believe the Lord is using Satan to fulfill His plans and purposes. The Lord is so masterful at turning the tables on Satan and this time is no different.

God used the world's COVID lockdown to recalibrate our focus on important values we had lost sight of, such as deepening our relationships within our homes and between kingdom families, strengthening our faith, and stretching our obedience.

We have learned so much about our relational shortcomings as a global church body and within our families. Hopefully, those values will stick with us long after the memories of COVID are gone. We need to make those learnings part of our everyday values by cherishing and honoring every relationship the Lord establishes. We can do that with our devotion and faithfulness to them. Those relationships are blessings from God's hand. We must ensure those relational values never die by instilling those values in our children and their children. Generational blessings come from our intentional teaching combined with the examples that we set with our everyday lives.

We know that God can take evil and turn it into good and we have all seen Him do that in our own lives.

Our nation is undoubtedly blessed by God's hand because of the covenant of our forefathers. Although much of our nation has turned away from God and His ways, the Lord is still with us. While His hand of judgment is upon us, it's only an attempt to draw our nation back into covenant with Jesus. I can almost hear the Lord cheering us on in Deuteronomy 30:2-10, reminding us of the covenant our forefathers made and how He yearns to delight in us once again.

> And when you and your children return to the Lord your God and obey him with all your heart and with all your soul according to everything I commanded you today, then the Lord your God will restore your fortunes and have compassion on you . . . He will make you more prosperous and numerous than your ancestors. The Lord your God will circumcise the hearts of your descendants, so that you may love him with all your heart and with all your soul, and live. The Lord your God will put all these curses on your enemies who hate and persecute you. You will again obey the Lord and follow all his commands I am giving you today. Then the Lord your God will make you most prosperous in all the work of your hands and in the fruit of your womb . . . The Lord will again delight in you and make you prosperous, just as he delighted in your ancestors [forefathers], if you obey the Lord your God and keep his commands and decrees that are written in the Book of the Law and turn to the Lord your God with all your heart and with all your soul.

Our heavenly Father is doing much more than He should to keep His end of the covenant our forefathers made with Him because God wants to resume pouring out His biggest blessings upon us for a thousand generations.

We possess an inheritance that the Lord provided to us when our forefathers established a covenant with God. Our inheritance is our families, our future, and our land. It is time we collectively tell Satan that he cannot have our inheritance. Let's take back the inheritance Satan stole.

The Word of God promises to bless our inheritance when we remain faithful to Him and His ways. Our journey back to a blessed land begins with obedience in the way we live and the way we lead within each facet of our culture. A blessed life is a choice between obedience to God's ways or sin. "This day I call the heavens and the earth as witnesses against you that I have set before you life and death, blessings and curses. Now choose life, so that you and your children may live and that you may love the Lord your God, listen to his voice, and hold fast to him. For the Lord is your life, and he will give you many years in the land he swore to give to your fathers" (Deuteronomy 31:19).

This God-moment goes much further than the borders of our own nation. This is a global move of God. The face of His church is being redefined, from our core values to the deepening of our faith; from the way we are bound in love with one another to the way we work together like a divine family. The Holy Spirit is maturing our understanding of His church, strengthening us and establishing deeper truths of God's Word within us.

Jesus is creating a beautiful bride capable of shining brightest during the darkest times—a bride who speaks truth through our words and our deeds. A truth that is saturated with the same love as that of our risen King. It is a type of love that causes the world to pursue His eternal truth amidst the pandemic of sinfulness. When we love to that degree, the world will see His beautiful bride in a different light, turning to her for justice and righteousness, during a time when such things cannot be found within the chaos of our world. That is the moment when the world will realize there is only one truth, and His name is Jesus Christ.

"Take to heart all the words I have solemnly declared to you this day, so that you may command your children to obey carefully all the words of this law. They are not just idle words for you – they are your life. By them you will live long in the land [that I, the Lord, have given you from my hand]" (Deuteronomy 32:46-48).

How can we start letting our light shine the brightest? Start searching for opportunities in the chaos. We will find opportunities within adversity if we maintain a kingdom perspective. Look for opportunities in people who advocate the horrors ravaging our land because amid great sin, there is even greater hurt, pain, and turmoil. Behind closed doors, within the secret lives of those responsible for causing the most violent crimes against humanity and against God, there is immense pain. Within all pain lie opportunities to share the love of Christ. Search for kingdom opportunities with a heavenly vantage point.

Ask the Holy Spirit to give you revelation to see kingdom opportunities, wisdom for strategies, and divine understanding to navigate through it all. Finally, I believe one of the most overlooked ingredients needed to make the most of your kingdom assignment is divine favor.

Dare to pray dangerous prayers that require blind faith, where trust in Jesus is our only possession. Prayers that will take us into the unknown where our most impactful assignments from the Lord exist. A realm of kingdom building that transcends time and leaves an eternal mark on our nation.

God's kingdom demands Jesus followers who are willing to sacrifice their own wants, needs and dreams for the advancement of biblical Christianity. Our world desperately needs Christians to develop a soldier-like mentality to fight in God's army, an army willing to fight for the eternal freedoms of our families, our nation's soul, and God's kingdom. These freedoms can only be gained through blood, sweat, and tears. Eternal freedom only comes by way of spiritual war, and it's our responsibility to fight this battle.

Start preparing yourself now. Think of your preparation like that of the special forces in the military. The Navy Seals employ a special training program called BUD/S Training. During the training, the Seals candidates learn to work together as an individual unit, where each individual learns to sacrifice their own needs, wants, and even their life. Candidates learn to push past their perceived limits of pain and suffering. They create a new threshold of endurance and resolve, while learning the true limits of their mental, emotional and physical capabilities. They develop a new mindset that ignores pain and bleeding, while running toward the most ferocious battles. Maintaining extreme focus and determination while accomplishing the mission for the good of the team is the only outcome that matters. Soldiers develop a mentality where enduring pain and suffering is expected, and surrender is not an option. And putting our life on the line to die for the cause is the ultimate honor.

Serving in our nation's military is a sacrifice and an honor. The soldier's entire family sacrifices, but our entire nation is free because of it. We should not be any different as Christians in God's army. In fact, our dedication, commitment, and willingness to find opportunities where we can sacrifice should become our sole purpose. After all, we are fighting a bigger war, where the eternal stakes are much higher, and our Commander is the King of all kings. The Creator of all things seen and unseen is at our helm. The Author of our very own eternal salvation is leading the charge. Jesus is leading a war that He declared against Satan and his army, while He

339

hung from the cross at Calvary and said, "It is finished" (John 19:30).

In God's army, the value of our lives should be measured against our willingness to lay it down for the mission of Jesus Christ. Our mentality of luxuries, comfort, and entitlement can no longer be a goal. That mentality should only be seen as an obstacle that holds us back from our ability to accomplish our Commander's mission . . . at all costs.

We were born for this special moment in history, a moment when our nation's destiny is at stake. Jesus created us for this moment in time to arise and take our destiny by the hand to move God's plans forward. This is the moment when our collective destinies collide with our nation's greatest purposes on earth. It's a collision of destinies that could prove to be our finest hour.

Don't let your biggest destiny slip away. Winston Churchill said something that resonates in the atmosphere today, and it applies to us right now. Winston said, "To each [person] there comes in their lifetime a special moment when they are figuratively tapped on the shoulder and offered the chance to do a very special thing, unique to them and fitted to their talents. What a tragedy if that moment finds them unprepared or unqualified for that which could have been their finest hour."

We have a rare opportunity to make a difference that helps shape the future for generations to come. How will you make the most of this moment? That's what our legacy is all about—impacting humanity for God in a way that grows stronger every generation. What legacy will we choose to leave? How will things end for us? Will our kids and grandkids live in a free country and a church filled with power and faith? Will Jesus and His ways become intolerable and completely removed from our society? Will the church sit back and allow the antichrist spirit to reign in our land?

Only God knows the answer to those questions. In the meantime, we can make a difference if each of us will find the courage to follow our biggest God-destiny by seeking the heart of God, so we can be part of His biggest plans for America.

If these words stir you, then you are chosen for this moment. His most significant work seen in our nation. Jesus is still writing the pages of the history of God's people and His church. Just what if you

341

were born for such a historical moment in the continued story of God's people? What if you have been chosen for God's greatest moment to turn around our nation and show the world about God's goodness? What if God birthed you at exact time and in the exact place that would prepare you for His greatest work?

Your life has the potential to convince the world about Jesus Christ and His grace that saves lives. While our nation is pulling away from God, there is an entire people pulling into God.

Allow God to mold you and make you more useful for His plans. Recalibrate your life and ministries to make God's plans your priority. Dare to follow the Holy Spirit's leading to redefine the status quo of the American church body. The advancement of Christianity is the very destiny we were born for. If we each place God's plans ahead of our own, together we will release the Holy Spirit in ways never before witnessed. Then the world will see how God turned around a corrupt nation, and it will assuredly give hope to all humanity. That's when America will become a beacon of light unto the world, and our collective destinies will be fulfilled through Jesus Christ.

Ask the Lord to grow your faith strong enough that one day, you will have the courage to say to Him, "I consider my life worth nothing to me; my only aim is to finish the race and complete the task the Lord Jesus has given me – the task of testifying to the good news of God's grace" (Acts 20:24).

Isaiah 60 is the church's anthem for advancing God's kingdom at this moment. Together, we shall recite and declare the verses in 1-3 and 21-22 over God's church, our nation and ourselves. "Arise, shine, for your light has come, and the glory of the Lord rises upon you. See, darkness covers the earth and thick darkness is over the peoples, but the Lord rises upon you and His glory appears over you. Nations will come to your light." "Then all your people will be righteous and they will possess the land forever. They are the shoot I have planted, the work of My hands, for the display of My splendor. The least of you will become a thousand, the smallest a mighty nation. I am the Lord; in its time I will do this swiftly."

This is our time, our land, and our destiny. We are the head and not the tail. Jesus placed us in charge of this world. Time to step up and never shrink back, to advance and never retreat, moving in the power of His divine family. We are the most holy possession of Jesus Christ. We are His church.

Lord, let Your face shine on us, keep Your hand on us, and deepen our faith. Create within us a deeper appetite for Your presence, a deeper love that binds our souls to Your ways because of Your unfailing love for us. Make us more useful to Your plans and purposes and help us to follow Jesus Christ with our very lives. Amen!

Today is our *Time to Stand.*

Endnote

[1] Wayne Jackson, "Is There Not A Cause?" ChristianCourier.com. Accessed June 27, 2021, at https://www.christiancourier.com/articles/1575-is-there-not-a-cause